MEN OF MARYKNOLL

MEN OF
Maryknoll

By
JAMES KELLER
and
MEYER BERGER

Essay Index Reprint Series

BOOKS FOR LIBRARIES PRESS
FREEPORT, NEW YORK

Library of Congress Cataloging in Publication Data

Keller, James Gregory, 1900–
    Men of Maryknoll.

    (Essay index reprint series)
    1. Catholic Foreign Mission Society of America
--Biography. I. Berger, Meyer, 1898–1959, joint
author. II. Title.
[BV2300.C35K4 1972]   266.2   78-142650
ISBN 0-8369-2775-3

PRINTED IN THE UNITED STATES OF AMERICA
BY
NEW WORLD BOOK MANUFACTURING CO., INC.
HALLANDALE, FLORIDA 33009

Contents

Prefatory Note

The stories of these Men of Maryknoll, as told in this volume, speak for themselves. They, like their fellowmen of Maryknoll, were plain Americans from farms, or factories, or mills, or mines, who chose the hard though rewarding career of missioners to serve their fellows in distant lands, physically as well as spiritually. Most of them serve in the Orient, though now Maryknoll has extended its field to South America. When the war came upon China and the Philippines, Men of Maryknoll had their part to play.

Maryknoll, from whence these men go out, overlooks the Hudson River near Ossining, about thirty miles from New York City. It came from a meeting of two American priests at the Windsor Hotel in Montreal in 1910,—a Bostonian, Father James Anthony Walsh, and a North Carolinian, Father Thomas Frederick Price. Both were deeply anxious to found a society to train young Americans for the Catholic mission fields of the world,—for at that time there was no organization in this country for that work. Pope Pius X gave them his approval in Rome on June 29, 1911, and this new society, given the formal title of Catholic Foreign Mission Society of America, was the result. Later the beautiful knoll in the Hudson Valley was chosen for its site. It was dedicated to the Virgin Mary, and so the name Maryknoll came to be.

JAMES KELLER

I

Connecticut Yankee
at Heaven's Gate

WHEN BIG JOE SWEENEY was a boy in New Britain in
Connecticut he didn't dream of living under Japanese
bombs and gunfire on a wild hillside in South China among
the walking dead—the ma fung lo, or "numb ones," which
is the Chinese name for lepers.

Big Joe was like any other New England kid. He fished
in Luther's and Larson's ponds for johnny roaches and
perch and pickerel. On Summer days he swam in Brophy's
Brook. In the Autumn he loved to tramp in the woods on
Pinnacle Mountain with his dog, and with his father who
was Joseph Patrick Sweeney, a grocer in New Britain.
They hunted foxes.

On Sundays when the grocery was closed Big Joe would
hitch Old Monk, a misnamed mare, to the family two-
seater buggy down at Foley's livery stable and he would
drive out into the country with Pat Hartney or Joe Hartney,
his cousins, sometimes with one of the girls who lived on
their block in Clark Street. On wet days he'd hide in the

1

barn and read *With Custer On The Plains,* or *Young Wild West and the Arapahoes.* His father did not approve such reading.

Big Joe committed most of the little boyhood sins. One day at St. Mary's School in New Britain, for example, Sister Boniface who was the strictest teacher in the senior grade decided that Joe was not pulling his weight in class. She gave a note to this effect to Joe Hartney to deliver to Bridget Oulihan Sweeney who is Joe's mother.

Joe Hartney is dead now, but he was a quiet, solemn sort of kid and loyal to Big Joe. They stopped behind the school yard to study Sister Boniface's note and figured it might upset Mrs. Sweeney. They filed it in a nearby sewer. When Mrs. Sweeney hadn't called a few days later, Sister Boniface, who knew boys, sent another and sharper note by one of Joe's three sisters. This note reached Mrs. Sweeney, and there was a grim conference.

Sister Boniface, grown old, never forgot the incident. When Big Joe came back to New Britain from China on furlough in 1932—he had been a Maryknoll Missioner for twelve years by this time—she cast it up to him. Big Joe, six feet three inches in height, worked his toes in his number twelves in sheer embarrassment and grinned sheepishly. He used to say, "Sister Boniface had that effect on you. She could always make you feel like a whipped pup."

There was, and still is, a lot of Tom Sawyer and something of Huck Finn in Big Joe. Father Leo Sweeney, who followed his older brother into Korea and China for Maryknoll, remembers the Summer day in their childhood when Joe walked the old wall on Shuttle Meadow Reservoir. A stone turned under Joe's foot and he splashed into the water. Swimming in the reservoir was forbidden but the afternoon was hot and, once in, Joe floated and swam until he was cooled. He was sixteen at the time but still under stern parental discipline.

Joe's clothes were wet when he got back to Clark Street. Mrs. Sweeney stopped him before he could get to his room. She said, "What happened, Joe?" and though he didn't mean to say it he blurted, "A little kid fell in the lake and I got him out." Mrs. Sweeney, like any mother, made Joe out a hero. She got him into dry clothes and proudly went among her neighbors downstreet and told them of the mythical rescue. When Leo wandered in around sundown he didn't know about Joe's impulsive whopper. Something he said betrayed Joe. Mrs. Sweeney was hurt, but not nearly so much as Joe was when his father got home. Mr. Sweeney had a horny palm for a grocer.

All this happened long ago. Big Joe Sweeney is forty-eight now and twenty-two of the years have been spent as a Maryknoll Missioner in Asia. He has lived ten years among the ma fung lo, a decade of extraordinary Christian devotion to helpless unfortunates. Throughout South China men speak with a certain awe of this follower of Damien. Even the Japanese who are supposed to fear nothing, keep their distance from Big Joe and his numb ones. Moreover they respect his courage. They cannot understand, though, why a white man should dedicate his life to Chinese, especially to the dread ma fung lo, but this is because, like most Orientals, they do not know enough about Christianity to understand Christian motives.

Missioners are apt to turn up on the stage or in fiction as

mealy-mouthed, hypocritical creatures and maybe there are such missioners. Big Joe, though, isn't the type. He's a giant American, cheerful, loves physical danger and adventure and sings at the grim work he has made his career. Men who have come upon his leper colony at Gae Moon— "Dangerous Door"—on West River Delta in the tropic South China Sea have stopped in astonishment at the weird swelling chorus that often rises shrill from the compound. It's Joe's favorite tune, one his father taught him:

> Proudly the note of the trumpet is sounding,
> Loudly the war cries arise on the gale;
> Fleetly the steed by Lough Suiling is bounding,
> To join the thick squadrons in Saimear's green vale.
> On every mountaineer,
> Strangers to flight and fear,
> Rush to the standard of Dauntless Red Hugh;
> Bonnought and Galloglass,
> Throng from each mountain pass,
> On for Old Erin—O'Donnell Abu!

"O'Donnell Abu" as the Cantonese ma fung lo sing it is, as you'd expect, startling and maybe a little incongruous, but they know—though they don't at all understand— all the countless verses of this Hibernian battle song. From Big Joe they've also picked up "Come Out Of The Kitchen, Mary Ann," and, "The Harp That Once Thro' Tara's Halls." Father Sweeney bawls the solo parts and the Cantonese join in the choruses as he works on their affected and distorted members.

Big Joe figures there are some hundreds of thousands of lepers in China. Before Maryknoll sent him to work among them, in 1933, they had small help and cold pity from the local people, a tradition of horror stood in the way. Dr. Dobson, a kindly Presbyterian missionary in Yeungkong, was one of the numerous Protestant missionaries whom Maryknollers saw showing them mercy; and Father Marsigny, a former Belgian aristocrat with a staff of Canadian nuns, cared for a large colony on Sheklung Island near Canton. Mostly, though, the afflicted huddled unattended in graveyards as Scriptural lepers did. They were often stoned, and in some rare cases shot or drowned, if they appeared too near a town or village or if they ventured onto a popular road or highway.

When Big Joe started his work in the Spring of 1933, he was sickened by the accounts of a recent leper massacre. "The first day I arrived here in Kwangtung," he wrote home, "I read that 100 lepers were shot by a squad of local military in a neighboring Province." At Pakkai an entire village turned out with scythes and guns and stones and threatened to herd sixty of the numb ones into the river to drown, but Big Joe heard of it and saved the unfortunates. Many of the simpler Chinese were a little puzzled by Big Joe's pity. They thought he was insane to work among the numb ones. The lepers themselves, oddly enough, were suspicious of him at first. "They think I am taking them in only to feed them the Black Bottle—poison, that is—and I must exercise extraordinary care," Big Joe wrote. "If one should happen to die during the first few days I would certainly be accused of his murder."

Big Joe had prepared long for his work among the ma fung lo. He had visited the Damien Colony on Molokai, and the United States Federal Leprosarium in Louisiana.

He had spent some time on Sheklung Island with Father Marsigny. He found a small colony of unfortunates uncared for and unattended in a banyan and bamboo grove at Sheung Yeung in South China.

"I entered the grove in broad daylight. Through the dusk made by overhanging boughs I followed a winding path to a clearing in the center. There I found ten adobe huts with thatched roofs. Sitting around in the dark were deformed creatures with only stumps where hands or feet should have been. Many had distorted faces. I saw an afflicted woman, hideous to behold, with a beautiful eight-months-old child in her arms. The child, as is often the case with the children of these unfortunates, was spotless."

Father Sweeney eventually cleaned out this spot and removed the ma fung lo from their bitter seclusion to the asylum he had set up in the extensive Sun Wui graveyards, near Kongmoon. From his Irish imagination and his Catholic faith he conjured for this weird haven the singularly appropriate name, "Gate of Heaven." The Chinese like the name, for they, like the Irish, have a great love for the poetic.

Big Joe got permission from the local magistrate in Toi Shaan to take over an abandoned Taoist Temple where a group of ma fung lo existed in utter despair and in indescribable squalor, with ancient idols frowning on them from the walls. He burned the sleeping mats and the boards that were beds, was liberal with disinfectant and with paint and used the temple, as he did the cleansed adobe huts in the banyan grove, for a receiving station. The cemeteries of Sun Wui remained his central station. About this time the Prefect of Yeung Kong, a helpful official, approached Big Joe with a proposition:

"He has offered an island at the mouth of Yeung Kong River as a central station," Big Joe wrote back to Maryknoll wistfully, "and this is a wonderful opportunity. Yet we dare not accept. He would present us with 200 cases right away and our finances do not permit us to take on such large numbers. It would be criminal to take them without funds to care for them. Some day, though, we'll get that island or some other island, possibly a corner of Sancian Island where St. Francis Xavier died. At the moment, however, the lepers we have tax our meagre resources."

Big Joe depended on contributions from friends of Maryknoll at home. When contributions were low, as they often were, he pulled his belt tighter, just as his patients did. When they were generous, Big Joe splurged on disinfectant, bandages and ethyl esters of Hydnocarpus Oil and Chaulmoogra Oil which he got from Culion in the Philippines at cost. These oils in some cases arrest the disease. Nothing has been found, through the centuries, that will cure it.

The Sz-Yap district to the south of Canton, incidentally, is the region from which we get most of our Chinese laundrymen, chop suey restaurant waiters and the population for Chinatowns in the United States.

Big Joe spent five years among the lepers in the Sun Wui cemeteries. With Big Joe labored Father Francis J. Connors of Peabody, Mass., a young priest who had come out to China in 1927, six years after Big Joe got there. Sun

Wui's gravelands, spread through the hills over many miles
north of the city, hold the sacred bones of countless generations of Chinese. When Big Joe took over some forty
or fifty lepers lived among the burial mounds. Lepers had
lived and died here for generations. The shelters were miserable shacks or lean-tos made of rotted coffin boards.
When nights were cold, the numb ones burned parts of
their shelters in the graveyard to keep warm.

No one, Big Joe found, came near them. When farmers
or other travellers passed on the road near the cemetery
the numb ones would slink out of sight. Most of the un-
afflicted in these South China regions believe that the ma
fung lo are victims of bad joss—evil omen—or of leprous
devils, or that they come by their ailment through eating
male fowl that have been capons less than three months and
four days. Descendants of lepers are often clean, especially
after the fourth generation, but in China the stigma of the
ma fung lo is nigh to eternal. There are entire villages of
clean folk descended from lepers but they carry an almost
insurmountable handicap in Chinese society.

In their graveyard colony in Sun Wui the ma fung lo,
when Big Joe came among them, lived chiefly on the few
dank vegetables they could nurse from the wet earth between burial mounds. Sometimes a farmer might throw a
cabbage or a handful of fruit over the crumbled cemetery
wall or leave food by the road where the ma fung lo might
creep down to get it after the benefactor had passed, but
mostly travellers—sometimes the very sons and daughters
of some of the afflicted—hurried fearfully past. The ma
fung lo were suffered to squat at isolated spots and beg
but seldom would they dare venture out to the wells to

drink. It was safer to slake their thirst with the muddy water that accumulated in graveyard depressions.

Big Joe knew exactly what he wanted to do when he went into the gravelands. He burned all the coffin-board hovels, the old boards that were beds and the grimy mats that covered them. He burned the lepers' clinging rags, the weeds around the shelters and the few pieces of crude furniture. The ma fung lo stood apart and stared in awe at this white giant who had dared come among them, but Big Joe was accustomed to such staring. Every new white missioner in China, especially in the upcountry where white men are rare, is stared at in the streets by the natives, adults as well as children. He gets used to having groups of naïve and highly curious Chinese encircle him to stare at his garments and his unusual features. He comes to expect them to discuss him excitedly among themselves, in his presence, as a group of scientists, say, might discuss some rare bug or insect. Of particular interest is the missioners' nose. The Chinese name for white men, in many provinces, is "the big noses." The Chinese nose is so snubby and small that a normal Western nose is something freakish in their sight. Big Joe, like other missioners, was even accustomed to having chant leaders of street work gangs make verses about him as he passed. Chinese chant leaders are great at extemporizing in this fashion. They'll sing, for example, "Here walks a foreigner. He has a lot of money in his pockets, but that is no help to us." As the chant leader raises his voice, all the coolies or laborers, heave on their ropes or their burdens in perfect rhythm, and grunt in assent.

Anyway, Big Joe accepted the frightened stare of the

Sun Wui ma fung lo as he did the goggling of Chinese at
street seminars. With lye and other strong disinfectants he
burned away all that was foul and evil, destroyed the rats
with poisons, and as fast as he tore down the shelters he
helped workmen put up new ones. First he erected temporary bamboo shacks covered with woven palm leaves. Later
he got enough money from home to put up sturdier buildings, some of mud brick, some with concrete floors. He
found some former artisans among his patients and distributed tools to them. Tears rolled down their cheeks. They
fondled saws, hammers and chisels as though they were
gifts beyond price. These were things they had never hoped
to handle again after they had fled their native hamlets
and villages. Eagerly they helped build a frame chapel, a
frame bungalow dispensary, kitchens and bathrooms. Big
Joe was touched by the artisans' joy at sight of ordinary
tools. "I had heard of men shedding tears of joy at the
restoration of a great work of art," he said, "but I had
never seen hammers and saws stir men to such deep emotionalism."

Father Connors was inclined to be grave, but Big Joe
sang at his work and the ma fung lo faces knew again how
to smile—distorted smiles, of course, but the first these
unfortunates had tried in years. By and by the lepers
caught onto the words of Big Joe's songs and wide-eyed
travellers would hear "On with O'Donnell, then! Fight the
old fight again! Strike for your country, O'Donnell Abu!"
Big Joe instituted a daily schedule, from daybreak through
dusk. There were prayers for the Christians among the
ma fung lo, though most of the lepers clung to their pagan
beliefs, then morning rice boiled over fires fed by dried

grass fuel and coffin boards, then medical treatment. Those who could labored in the truck and flower gardens in the graveyard.

Within a few months the Chinese beggars' grapevine carried over this region of South China the legend of the *hung mo Kwai*, or "red haired devil," (another Chinese term for a white man) who was restoring life to the numb ones in the Sun Wui gravelands. Moving by night, when there was less risk of insult or arrest, other lepers journeyed toward Sun Wui to partake of this miracle. They'd lay up in cemeteries through the daylight hours, then crawl or hobble through the dark to the next cemetery before sunup. Some came hundreds of miles by these graveyard jumps. Big Joe took in all he could, but when the buildings were filled he'd turn the surplus away, though it hurt to do it. He wired to Maryknoll in New York to get him more sponsors and little by little "The Gate of Heaven" colony expanded.

When Spring came to Sun Wui in 1934, the ma fung lo settlement in the gravelands was transformed. Before Big Joe had moved in, Spring and Summer found the place aswarm with rats and clouds of noisy flies, the coffin-board shelters rotten and thick with filth, the water and the meagre food—the very air about the colony—loathesome to sickening degree. Now, one year later, the new huts were clean and shining in the warm sun, transplanted banana, papaya and orange blossoms sweetened the air. Green hedges flourished and made compound walls. Paths were bordered with flower beds and the lepers' eyes were delighted with the lush beauty of azaleas, peonies, hibiscus, bell flowers and rhododendron. The flowers attracted birds and the gravelands haven was enriched with their song. Big Joe had wrought a miracle.

Through the first five years the colony steadily expanded until it held several hundred of the ma fung lo. Father Sweeney was able to buy greater quantity of medicine from Culion as word of his work drifted home to the United States, through Maryknoll. As the contributions swelled, he extended shelter and hospital facilities and took in more and more of the afflicted. Dr. Harry Blaber, a surgeon from Brooklyn, who operated a small mission hospital in Toi Shaan, volunteered his services and helped with the patients once a week. A Dr. J. J. Sherry, a Dublin man who had been a surgeon with the British Army, added his skill and knowledge for more than a year before age and failing health compelled him to give up. Dr. Artemio Bagalawis, a nephew of General Aguinaldo the Filipino Napoleon, who had studied leprosy in the Philippines, came as a volunteer in 1936, just after the venerable Dr. Sherry had to leave. Big Joe saw in these replacements the hand of God.

There were deaths in the colony from time to time, but much fewer than there had been before Big Joe had started his work. New patients literally waited at the cemetery hedges to take the beds of the ma fung lo who were buried. The waiting line was never empty—probably never will be. Some of the patients were withered crones and Chinese patriarchs who had known great wealth and high position, and some had always been beggars and vagabonds, but Gate of Heaven knew no distinction. Big Joe was aware that high station and wealth, poverty and low birth alike were levelled by the stigma of the ma fung lo and that neither the rich nor the poor could stay in their native communities once their blight was discovered. "All lepers in China are treated like those of the Old Testament," Big Joe tells you. "Their usual lot is to be shunned and cast out and left to die."

One morning Big Joe and his patients heard a great outcry beyond the gravelands compound, the swelling angry chorus of a mob. Big Joe, a giant in white doctor's garb, got up from a treatment, and peered into the road. He saw a little girl about eight years old, kept moving by two big Chinese policemen who prodded her with long bamboo poles. Healthy Chinese children of various ages shrilled insults at her from a distance and cried the shameful epithet "Ma fung!" "Ma fung!" The child was barefoot. Her little feet, her legs and her tiny face were caked with dust. Her face bore no leper's mark, but tears had marked their course in the grime on her cheeks. She wore tattered and faded blue cotton pantaloons and in her hand, done up in a cloth, she carried all she owned—a rice bowl and a pair of chopsticks.

The policemen and the shrill tormentors fell back when Big Joe came into the road and dropped to one knee before her. "It was the only time I knew her to cry," he'd say later. The child stared at him in wonder. She had never seen a white man before. She could not understand his kindness. Big Joe said in Chinese, "Who are you, little girl?" and she answered "I am a leper." Big Joe's own eyes brimmed over as he looked into her dark eyes. He studied the spotless, flower-like face, but the child's right hand and forearm were deformed in an unmistakable way. Ah Chai was of the ma fung lo.

Big Joe took her by the hand, and the policemen and the other tormentors muttered and dispersed. They could not understand this giant ghost man. Big Joe led the child along the flowered graveland paths and let her tell her story. She could not remember her father or mother, nor her brothers and sisters, though she knew she came of a large family. She had been sold as a *mui tsai*, a slave girl, to the Wongs. In China the Wongs are more numerous than Smiths or Joneses in the United States, so the name meant nothing. She had been hand-servant to Grandmother Wong and she had been taught to cook and to scrub. A visitor to the Wongs had noticed the deformed hand and had detected it for what it was. Wong servants had immediately rushed Ah Chai out of the house and had led her many leagues to Sun Wui and had abandoned her there, in the streets. She did not know the name of the town where the Wongs lived. In Sun Wui the mob had discovered her and had called the police. This was her story, told in simple childish treble.

"Somehow," Big Joe says, when he talks of Ah Chai, "she made me think of St. Agnes. She was a normal kid, yet there was something about her, some spiritual quality, that softened all who knew her."

The grimmest and most hardened vagabonds among the lepers of Sun Wui, and there were some tough old curmudgeons among them, could not be cold to Ah Chai. When she moved happily down the flowered cemetery paths, they smiled their distorted smiles at her and the sun of her smile beamed on them. Incidentally, Ah Chai's face remained clean and spotless though the disease moved up her arm and twisted it out of shape, in spite of all treatment. She was assigned to minister to the bedridden in the Sun Wui gravelands and her little tasks kept her trotting through the long days. After the moment of her rescue no one ever saw her cry again, though she suffered intense pain and was shaken, at times, by searing fever.

The lepers of Sun Wui, not the priests, came to think of Ah Chai as a little saint. Dressed in fresh clothes—made-overs, fashioned by crippled fingers from secondhand garments sent across the ocean by friends of Maryknoll—she moved among the stricken, always cheerful and innocent. Big Joe and Father Connors would scold her, sometimes, in mock gruffness, but Ah Chai understood and always smiled back. Big Joe, for example, would say, when he assigned her to care for old Mrs. Foon who was blind and hopelessly crippled, "Mother, if Ah Chai is not a good hand-maiden and if she does not treat you gently, you must take a stick and beat her soundly." Ah Chai would smile but Mrs. Foon, out of her darkness would speak of the child in warm praise. She would assure Big Joe that Ah Chai was the most gentle of nurses, which he knew.

Ah Chai lived less than three years after Big Joe saved her from the mob. She died, oddly enough, not of leprosy but of leukemia. Big Joe and the doctors gave her their most tender care, but they could not save her. One afternoon, as Summer sun glowed pink on the azaleas and on the melancholy burial mounds of Sun Wui, the child smiled up at Big Joe from her cot, her cheeks aglow with fever. Her small fingers tightened on his great ones. She

turned her face to the bamboo wall and fell asleep, forever.
Big Joe sobbed as the leper nurses with tears trickling
crookedly down their knobbed features, drew the white
sheet over Ah Chai's face.

Her funeral was remarkable for Sun Wui. The ma fung
lo were accustomed to death and burials were common.
At Ah Chai's funeral, though, every last man and woman
crowded around and Big Joe and Father Connors both
noticed that callous old leper beggars and the hardest
vagabonds from China's roadsides and city streets, were
bowed in grief. Christian prayers and pagan supplication
mingled at the child's grave. When the service was ended
and the ma fung lo shuffled back to the bamboo huts, the
women wept. Lin Cheung, who had been a fisherman in
the China Sea before the disease compelled him to leave
his wife and children, uttered their common thought from
the wisdom of his seventy years. Lin Cheung said, "God
has plucked our pretty flower."

Every numb one in Big Joe's colony had a touching
story which would unfold little by little, under his tender
ministration. Oldest of all his flock was a white-haired
woman, close to ninety, whose mutilated features, by some
unaccountable Divine artistry, still told of past beauty. In
the colony she was called Lo Mo, which is Chinese for Old
(Venerable) Mother. She had lived, near as Big Joe could
figure, some eighteen years in the Sun Wui gravelands,
ever staring through Death's door, yet clinging, somehow,
to life. When Big Joe came to Sun Wui, Lo Mo was foot-
less, without fingers and totally blind.

Lo Mo never told Big Joe her name. Her husband
(though she didn't know if he still lived) and her two

sons and one daughter would lose face if their townsfolk were to learn that Lo Mo, their kin, was of the ma fung lo. Indeed, she told the priest, she had left them and her beloved household so that not even they knew.

"It is not because of vanity, Good Father," she told Big Joe, "that I tell you that in my girlhood and when I was a young mother, I was known for my beauty. My husband was a man of wealth. When we married I went, as is our custom, to live with his people and I bore him two sons and a daughter. There was joy in our house and my husband and I looked toward a future of ripe years with our children and their children to brighten the years."

One night when Lo Mo worshipped at the household shrine and prayed to the family ancestors for blessings on her home, her arm passed through the flame of a scented candle. The arm blistered, but, curiously, there had been no pain. Lo Mo knew a sudden fear, but dared not voice it. Many weeks later, shadowy patches blossomed where the candle had burned, discolorations that resembled ring-worms. She treated these secretly with lotions and magic writings, but the patches spread and numbness and occasional prickling "like pins and needles" stirred under them. Worry and sleepless nights, spent in trying to decide her course, brought the disease to rapid flowering.

Lo Mo told Big Joe how she left her bed during one of these restless nights and how she stood for a few brief moments over her slumbering children. She took the household funds and in the dark night started blindly down the highway to Canton. In Canton, Lo Mo managed, for a while to conceal her ailment, but when her money was gone and after she had sold her jewels and her finery, she went on the street as a beggar. She came, by slow stages, to the gravelands of Sun Wui, and here she had lived through the long years. She told Big Joe that many nights she dreamed of her old home, so different from the coffin-board shelter and the grimy mats on the damp cemetery soil, but never ventured near it. She often thought of ending her life, but something always kept her from it.

"Only once," Lo Mo told Big Joe proudly, "did I weaken. One night before I lost the use of my legs completely and before my fingers were gone, I could not resist the desire to look at least once again on my home and my children. I covered my sores and I took to the road."

Lo Mo found every foot of the way an almost unbearable agony. She slept at night in abandoned temples, or on the outer rim of beggars' dry-grass campfires. Chinese beggars, it seems, are eager gossips. They mouth over every old legend and every scrap of news they may seize upon. At one campfire, Lo Mo, in the shadow, heard re-told the story of her own mysterious vanishment. Her husband, she learned, had re-married, her eldest son had taken a wife. Outside her native village, by the road, her heart pounded when her husband passed. He was, she assured Big Joe, tall and handsome and of noble bearing.

"But I shall be forever glad that I had strength of heart and of mind not to call out to him," the blind old lady told the priest. "He looked in my direction, but he did not know me. I thought my heart would leap through my throat."

Within the next few days, Lo Mo saw one of her former household servants pass toward the market. This woman did not know her, but tossed a coin at her feet. Lo Mo still sat by the road. She had heard, among the beggars, that her daughter had married a man of the town and that she was nursing a child of her own.

"This I would have died to see," Lo Mo told Father Sweeney. "This would have repaid me for all my years of loneliness. This, you understand, would have brightened the remainder of my years at Sun Wui. It would have been seed for good dreams."

Lo Mo never saw her daughter, nor her grandchild. A policeman noticed the patches on her arms. She was prodded and pushed from her roadside watching place. She crawled back to the gravelands. She had been there ever since.

"But I was happy, Good Father," she told Big Joe. "I cried, but I wept for joy that I had not made my sacrifice for nothing. They whom I most loved had never learned of my ailment. They had never learned why I vanished. They are not cursed with the stain of the ma fung lo, nor shall they ever be."

Lo Mo died at Gae Moon in 1940.

From Sun Wui a Chinese husband came one day to Gate of Heaven to ask that Big Joe take in his wife. For fifteen years her family had kept her locked in a darkened room, but finally word of the family's secret had seeped through Sun Wui and noisy mobs had come to the house to demand that she be cast out. Big Joe had no room, but the story touched him. He said he would take the woman. Along the road, next day, came a strange procession. The afflicted woman had refused to leave her room. She had been stirred out with poles by the local constabulary, ropes had been cast over her and she was led and dragged to

Sun Wui as cattle are led to market. A few hours later a bright-faced lad in his 'teens came to Big Joe, outside of Sun Wui chapel. He wanted to look at the woman. "She is my mother," he told the padre. With some twenty feet between them, mother and son stared at each other in anguish and the tears flowed freely down their cheeks. He left the compound still blinded with tears.

Lin Cheung the fisherman, who had been born on a boat as had most of his forefathers before him, was one of the characters of Sun Wui. All his life Cheung had known only clean ocean winds and glorious starry nights. He had raised his family on his junk, had kept them well fed and content with his cheerful labor. One day, though, a fish buyer in port detected tell-tale patches on Lin Cheung's arms and had spread the word. Rather than cause his comely wife and brood to lose face, Lin Cheung had left them. He had moved inland, always at night, with his sea bag and one oar for burden. Big Joe took him in. Wherever Cheung went in the gravelands, he always carried the oar. It was to him the symbol of the pleasant life he had left behind. He hated life ashore and willingly yielded to the inroads of the plague. When he died, late in the Autumn of 1937, Big Joe laid him to rest and—such is the sentimental understanding of the Irish—tenderly placed the cherished oar beside him.

Big Joe was sorely tried through the first years, in spite of his advances at Sun Wui. Sometimes the heat, as in the Summer of 1936, was virtually unbearable. Tropical sun burned into the palm-thatched huts and graveyard dampness mildewed the shelters. Shoes, garments and supply boxes acquired the mildew fungus. Mosquitoes sometimes attacked in clouds, despite all attempts to destroy them. Flies could be brushed off the priests' arms, they swarmed so thickly. The older ma fung lo withered, and dropped away. After Cheung was laid to rest with his oar, death took Wong King San, an ancient farmer and Lin Sho, an octogenarian rattan worker and Chan Cheung, who had been a man of some wealth in a hamlet near Canton. Another old man died violently insane. It was disheartening. Big Joe and Father Connors had to serve as doctors, priests and undertakers. They found no time for rest.

"Father Connors and I went down but only for the short count," Big Joe wrote home a few months later. "This is not an admission that we cannot take it. Even the Chinese farmers in this region found the days so hot that they harvested their rice by lamplight and even people who had good homes, slept in their gardens or in the streets."

When Summer's hot breath subsided and cooling Autumn brought relief, the work went more smoothly.

"I wish you could see the change in the lives of these derelicts of the roadside and the cemeteries," Big Joe informed Maryknoll at home, "especially in the child lepers and in the old folk. Tonight, for example, I look down on a village in the heart of the cemeteries and find it one of the most cheerful in China. It is one of the cleanest and has more flowers in it, for its size, than any that I know. Some of my people are suffering at the gate of the next world, but they know now that beyond lies eternal joy."

By this time Big Joe had a modern laboratory in the graveyard, and places for records of each patient's bacteriological tests, blood tests. He had good microscopes and fair medical equipment. The International Journal of Leprosy mentioned Sun Wui colony even then as a "leading institution" and in St. Louis, before the Medical Section of the American Association for the Advancement of Science, Perry Burgess of the American Leprosy Foundation praised Big Joe's dispensary and outpatient work with unusual warmth. "I found," he told the convention, "a clinician and bacteriologist with modest but inadequate laboratory equipment and examinations being made and treatment given with extreme care and intelligence.

After Big Joe had toiled three years in the Sun Wui cemeteries the Chinese Government, impressed by the miracle he had achieved there, ceded to Gate of Heaven Leprosarium more than 300 virgin acres at Gae Moon, 30 miles South of Sun Wui and at the mouth of Kongmoon River. This wild spot on the South China coast, remote from important communities, was ideal for the purpose and Big Joe pleaded with Maryknoll in New York to get him enough money to move his numb ones from the gravelands, and to prepare permanent quarters for them at the site in the wilderness. He had exultant dreams, then, of setting up durable accommodations for at least one thousand of the ma fung lo, possibly for several thousand over a stretch of years.

It called for dangerous pioneering, but Big Joe welcomed that, as, when he first went to Asia, he had eagerly taken up the challenge of travel in Manchuria near the Siberian border when the temperature was fifty below and his catechist froze to death on the trail. Big Joe left Father Connors in charge of the gravelands colony while he went with hired Chinese laborers and some of his leper artisans to clear ground at Gae Moon. Throughout torrid July and August, 1937, he worked with them cutting roads, built a temporary pier to unload bricks and other building materials, and laid out the sites for his hospital, church, and leper dwellings, for orchards and for truck gardens. He waded into the bush with the laborers, killing snakes, fighting insect swarms, and got up the first few buildings.

At midnight, September 2nd, a typhoon struck. Big Joe and the laborers sat up in their beds as a keening wind suddenly banged the windows and tore at the roofs of their dwellings at Gae Moon. Workers' matsheds blew away and slapped against the mountainside. In the stronger mud brick buildings wind drove rain through the walls. Father Sweeney told later how the rain boiled through every crack and window and came hissing through the floor tiles. "Tiles came loose and washed away like autumn leaves." Through the night the wind increased and just before dawn it reached a velocity of 164 miles an hour, the worst recorded typhoon of those parts. Stagings crashed, big boards sailed across the clearing like so much legal parchment. The pier carried away. The river towered in enormous angry waves and roared across the flat land. An enormous motor launch was carried from the landing hundreds of feet into the fields. Big Joe, for all his 220 pounds, was beaten to his hands and knees and with Brother Albert, his assistant, lay flat on the ground as the typhoon shrieked and tore at them. "We thought if we tried to stand we might soar like swallows," Big Joe recounted later, "so we stayed on our hands and knees, hugging the soil. Flying pebbles and stem bits peppered our skin like needles." They worked around crabwise until the typhoon, at dawn, went shrieking inland.

They found their laborers and leper artisans lying flat under their collapsed sheds, none seriously hurt but all highly frightened of the wind devils.

At Sun Wui Father Connors got the same dose, in spades, as the saying goes. He awoke to a night filled with the terrified shrillness of women patients, the hoarse cries of the men. Every building in the gravelands collapsed. At dawn everything was beaten into the cemetery earth and Father Connors spent four hours pulling the dying and the helpless from under the bamboo shed debris. He said "Our poor lepers stood in the wind and the rain and shivered. Their cooking utensils, rice bowls, beds and kitchen were destroyed. The firewood was so soaked we could not start a fire to warm them or to cook rice. I tried to buy hot rice gruel in the town, but it could not be had at any price. The poor unfortunates suffered intensely, but I heard no word of complaint. We now have the task of rebuilding the whole asylum. It is a bit discouraging."

Trouble came double at this period. The sheds were barely replaced before the Japanese made war. Their bombers came over Canton and Sun Wui. Big Joe and Father Connors herded their pitiful wards into the cemetery hollows as the gravelands shuddered and rocked under the bombs' impact. None of the lepers was hit.

In mid-Summer, the following year, Big Joe moved his 300 ma fung lo from the gravelands to the new settlement. As he led them aboard hired junks for the trip the populace of Sun Wui watched from afar and marvelled. Scores of the afflicted who were not of the colony, but only out-patients, stood on the banks, and, stared wistfully at the embarking ma fung lo bound, as they put it, "To the Numb

Ones' Paradise." Zeros and Jap bombers were frequently in the sky, above Sun Wui at this time, ready to machine gun or plaster anything that moved on Kongmoon River, but at dusk Big Joe gave the signal to start and the little fleet moved out with the ma fung lo huddled on the decks. Two of the eight junks were attacked from the air, but the bombs splashed into the sea. The entire contingent landed unharmed.

At daybreak, when the ma fung lo looked upon the new Gate of Heaven they were shrill with joy. Birds flashed and sang everywhere. Here were no dismal burial mounds, no melancholy swamps and hollows. The air was fresh and clean under the tropic sun. Overhead, that morning, they saw the "great silver bird," the Pan-American Clipper northbound from Manila, banking gracefully as it made the turn over the South China Sea. The sky above their little delta was the clipper's pivot point. From their little sandy beach they could look out upon snubby junks and bat-winged sampans. The child lepers could run and play on the sand and within a week they were golden-brown sprites knowing a freedom and joy they had never known before.

Behind the delta, mountains soared toward blue heaven. In the good earth papaya trees were rich with fruit and sprawling banyans flourished. Azaleas and hibiscus grew in profusion here and peach and apricot trees, brought down from the Sun Wui district and transplanted the previous Fall, had taken hold to make pleasant orchards. They had clear drinking water from the sparkling mountain springs. The gardens were ready and the lepers—those who could walk, at least—delighted in tending the goat herds, the ducks and the hens. Ah Chen, who had been a laundryman in Chicago but had contracted leprosy after he came home to live off his American-earned riches, laid out a field where he was to teach the child lepers to play ball. There was ample fish in the river.

The ma fung lo inspected their new brick homes first in silent awe, then filled the air with excitable shrill comment. The brick dorms had comfortable cots and each room was made to hold eight men or eight women. The roofs were sturdy, set on stout ridges. The windows were screened against insects and the floors were spotless concrete instead of graveland soil. The church had regular pews, an altar with a bronze tabernacle made by Brother Albert, and an organ, and the sun streamed warmly through pink and golden panes set in by the leper artisans. The interior glowed with their color. Behind the chapel there was a modern dispensary, better equipped than the cemetery's had been. No wonder that tears stood in the Numb Ones' eyes when they saw the giant Connecticut Yankee. They blessed this *Shen Fu,* their priest, when he so much as crossed their path, though many of them had never become Christians, but clung to their pagan beliefs.

Soon after the transfer from Sun Wui, Father Connors went back to the United States, on furlough. He stayed a while in Maryknoll's great stone dwelling on the Hudson near Ossining in New York, and then went to Misericordia Hospital in Philadelphia. On the morning of February 3, 1939, the Mother Superior at the hospital sent word to Maryknoll that Father Connors was dying. A priest who had known him through boyhood through his seminary days at Maryknoll sat by his bed. Father Connors murmured from the remote rim of consciousness, "Goodbye,

I'll see you in Heaven. . . . . I have never been afraid
to die. . . . . I hope that I have never hurt anyone." The
priest who had shared his childhood spoke brokenly: "De-
part, Christian soul." Big Joe heard the news at Heaven's
Gate with leaden heart. Maryknoll sent Father Joseph
Farnen of Baltimore, a smaller Joe, to take up where
Father Connors had left off and the Shen Fus of Gae Moon
are known throughout South China now as Big Joe and
Little Joe.

Japanese invasion of China had beset Big Joe's project
with new difficulties. The Japanese moved a contingent into
a fort opposite the Gate of Heaven at Gae Moon and shots
from the fort now endangered leper lives. Big Joe was
helpless against this, but if the Japanese expected him to
quit they didn't know this Connecticut Yank. Two of his
goatherds were wounded by rifle fire. He tended them and
restored them to their herds. Heedless of the enemy he
celebrated Mass each morning—and still does—even
though Japanese rifles and small cannon use his compound
for target practice. When their planes come over, as they
sometimes do, Big Joe leads his afflicted into caves in the
mountain and cares for them there. He has set up an altar
in the caves and a secondary dispensary, with a communi-
cating trench to protect his people from Japanese gunfire
as they move from the buildings to the caverns.

In August of 1941, Big Joe hired Chinese blockade
runners to help them get in a year's supply of medicines,
drugs and goods. Desperate refugees had poured over the
South China roads, seeking any avenue of escape from the
Japanese and hundreds had, somehow, found their way to
the Gate of Heaven, a spot they would ordinarily have

shunned. In addition to his ma fung lo, Big Joe had some 500 visitors whom he could not turn away, men and women of virtually all nations. These he had to feed. It was imperative that he get the supplies through, at any risk. He loaded his Chinese blockade runner at Macao, a neutral port, and on the night of August 27 headed home through darkness.

A Japanese cutter hailed Big Joe's craft out of the black night but the Chinese crew pushed their cabin cruiser harder. The Japanese searchlight found them, machine gun slugs spattered on the cabin. The Chinese returned the fire and the Japanese dropped astern, but only momentarily. Off To Fuk, about one hour from Gae Moon, the cutter closed in again and more machine gun fire was exchanged. Tracers hem-stitched darkness. As the craft drew together, the Chinese threw grenades on the cutter's deck. The Japanese, with wounded sprawled on their decks, charged and rammed the cabin cruiser. Big Joe realized then that his supplies were done for, but he could not risk capture. He could not stay away from Gate of Heaven.

He slipped out of his garments, ready to dive if the Japanese should board his blockade runner. A few minutes after the ramming, while the hand-to-hand fighting raged, a second Japanese cutter bore down out of the darkness. Big Joe put his passport into his shorts and slid over the side into the warm South China Sea. He swam through gloom. This was different, though, from floating in Larson's Pond or Shuttle Meadow Reservoir. Japanese lights swept the sea and he had to duck several times to avoid it. Big Joe was in the water six hours. At daylight he sighted

Ko Lan, a tiny uninhabited island. He swam to it and fell on the sand into the deep sleep of utter exhaustion.

When Big Joe stirred from his slumber, he was burned red by the sun, a sort of giant Robinson Crusoe with thinned brown hair, shoeless and clad only in his shorts. He found no food on the island, but a stream of clear water quenched his parched throat. On the third day, an old Chinese fisherman and his son came to the island. They stayed ten days. At Gate of Heaven there was great sorrow. The ma fung lo were desolate. On September 7, though, a messenger slipped ashore at Gae Moon. He reported that the fisherman had brought Big Joe to Kan Po Shek, just upriver, and there was rejoicing in the colony. Father John Joyce, a Maryknoll man whose father is a battalion fire chief in New York City, landed at Kan Po Shek with shoes and clothing and Big Joe returned to Gate of Heaven. He was red from the sun and his scant hair was bleached almost white, but the ma fung lo wept for joy at sight of him. Big Joe's reaction was characteristic. He laughed as he contemplated what the Japanese cutter crew must have thought when they found his shoes and his clothes on the blockade runner's deck. "My number twelves must have made their eyes pop," he told Father Joyce. "They'll either put them in a museum in Tokyo or maybe they're using them for landing barges."

II

Iowa Plowman

ONE OF CHINA's most extraordinary missioners is an Iowa plowman who actually harvests souls on a farmer's formula. This agricultural approach has worked with remarkable success in the spiritual field. By the farmer's method Father Bernard F. Meyer has perhaps garnered more converts, performed more baptisms and built more missions than any other American missioner in South China. After the Japanese took Hong Kong his internment camp truck gardens saved children, soldiers and civilians from death through malnutrition. On the literary side, his Cantonese-English dictionary was standard for the English-speaking wanderers in Southeastern China.

Farm-bred and enthusiastically devoted to the soil, he was convinced when he first entered the missions in 1918, that pagan lands are no different from a new field in which a farmer wants to prepare, say, for corn. "New land," he mused in print, "requires years of cultivation. You turn the sod and try to kill out the old weeds and grass roots. In this case the only difference is that it's superstitions and pagan beliefs instead of grass and weeds. To prevent re-rooting, you keep cultivating and by and by you obtain perfect tilth. Then you sow your seed and the seed is God's word. Your crops are bound to thrive."

It was characteristic of Bernard Meyer that, having worked out a formula, he should labor at it with superhuman energy. His mission hours, even after a quarter century, are pretty much like any hard-working farmer's, on most days considerably longer. His almost frightening energy has astonished even the tough coolies of South China, who are accustomed to working like draught animals. Over and over again, on long journeys into the mission fields to get in his soul crop, the plowman from Iowa has left them physically exhausted while he remained nowheres near spent.

Nature equipped Bernard Meyer for prodigious feats of both agricultural and spiritual husbandry. He stands five feet eight inches in height, has an awesome shoulder span, legs like oak stumps. His hands, developed by years of hand-milking on his father's acres in Stuart, Iowa, are enormous. Even the Chinese, who customarily shrill all street conversation—even delicate family secrets—are abashed at their own inadequacy after they have heard the plowman's remarkably penetrating voice.

They call the plowman missioner Ma Shen Foo, literally the Spiritual Father Meyer. "Ma" is as close as they seem to come to saying "Meyer." Wherever he has worked in South China, natives have come to regard him with extreme affection despite his terrible gravity and seemingly inexhaustible energy. When he left Kochow to start a new mission in Hoingan in October, 1923, his reputation preceded him. A Chinese banner proclaimed "Glad Welcome," at Hoingan Gate, and strings of bursting fireworks marked his sturdy progress up crooked little alleys to the new headquarters.

Father Meyer was born on February 16, 1891, in Brooklyn, Iowa, on a 160-acre farm. Father Meyer's parents were of German stock. He worked the fields, herded and milked cows and performed man-size chores when he was barely wagon-hub height. One evening when he was about thirteen, he retired to the hay loft with a biography of the French Missioner Just de Bretenières. At supper he quietly announced, "I'll be a missioner." His parents were mildly astonished, but they knew that this decision was as final as it was sudden. After Bernard got through the district parochial school and St. Ambrose College in Davenport, and spent some years at St. Mary's Seminary, Baltimore, he entered Maryknoll in August 1914.

Maryknoll today is an imposing edifice of gray stone on lovely Sunset Hill, staring westward across the Tappan Zee, eight miles to the Palisades. When Bernard Meyer clumped in, it was a collection of weathered and leaky gray farm buildings, set in tangled woods. The handful of seminarians shivered through severe Winters. The founder, James Anthony Walsh, had to skip a few notes on the tiny portable organ at service every now and then, to warm numbed fingers at an oil stove set at his elbow for the purpose. Pioneering was combined with study, but pioneering brought out Bernard Meyer's special talents.

The men on Sunset Hill who were to be Maryknoll's shock troops in China, were the first to marvel at the Iowa plowman's horse power. He cleared scrub, felled trees, cleared garden space, planted enough vegetables to more than fill their needs, set out orchards. He built fences, carved altar candlesticks, improved the cow herd. He sold the original flock of scrub chickens and replaced them with barred Plymouth rocks that gave not only eggs, but were broad-chested and generally better fleshed for eating. His way with fowl won him the nickname "Chick," which stays with him.

He tramped the country-side to study barns and finally conceived an improved barn design. Under his driving power the other men—one a lad from the steel mills, the other city boys—raised a mansard-roofed barn that rivalled anything in that part of Westchester County and gave shelter and feed space for forty head. Beside it he raised a gigantic silo for Winter feed. These structures, the orchard and the gardens are still in use, twenty-five years later. Like the man who built them they show no sign of wear, but look as though they might stand forever.

It was the same with academic and ecclesiastic studies. Father Meyer was not a brilliant student, but he ground away at his notes and books and warmed instruction over and over again in his mind as the earth warms seed to germinate it. This was the hard way, but once the seed took root, this farmer grimly nurtured and cultivated it for maximum yield. His genius for all agriculture, even mental, was astounding. His basic formula never failed.

When the first four Maryknoll men went to South China in the Winter of 1918, the task of the Church in China was staggering. German, Italian and French missioners whose funds and supplies had stopped when their native lands concentrated on the war had watched the fields they had plowed—so Father Meyer thought of it—fast yielding

again to the hungry weeds and grass roots of Oriental superstition. These fields were the home of 400,000,000 souls.
The veteran European missioners received the Americans
with frank misgivings. "Americans are too soft for this
work," they said. They didn't know about the Iowa plowman.

Father Meyer s intensely practical nature was irritated,
at first, by centuries-old, unchanging Chinese labor
methods. His first letters from the mission area virtually
boiled over at thought of the wasted human energy he encountered on every hand. Six coolies patiently raising and
dropping a huge iron hammer to drive a piling, old women
and children patiently breaking granite into small stone
by chipping with little hammers, crews pulling buckets up
hand over hand to raise sand from the water—these primitive processes were all but sacrilegious in Father Meyer's
sight. He was to accept them—somewhat grumpily, it's
true—as part of an aged tradition, but wherever he took
charge he managed, somehow, to work up a little more
speed. He was a little envious, though, of certain Chinese
work talents he couldn't imitate:

"Saw Chinese carpenter on roof slip off his clogs and
hold work with his toes while his hands were busy," he
wrote. A footnote conceded: "This has obvious advan-
tages."

The Chinese language puzzled him at first. "There are
some 780 basic words, or signs," he mused, "each sub-
ject to change of meaning with each of nine different voice
tones. In addition there are many aspirated and unaspir-
ated consonants and long and short vowels. Wrong tone,
wrong word." This gave some of the young American mis-

sioners mental goose-pimples, but not the Iowa farmer. He
set his mind's plow-share to this linguistic glebe and kept
at it. Today he is an outstanding master of the Chinese
language in the American missions. His Cantonese-American dictionary is a mission's classic.

Father Meyer buttonholed Chinese in the narrow streets
of Tungchen within six months of his arrival in the country,
and brashly engaged natives in conversation in their own
tongue. Nine times out of ten they understood little, or no
part of his Iowa Cantonese, but he made headway and
could drive a hard bargain at the little Chinese shops while
most of the other missioners were still floundering with
syllables. He preached his first sermon in Chinese in Tungchen chapel on Christmas, 1919, barely a year after his
arrival in South China. "Made my bow as a preacher today" his diary faithfully recorded. "The blank looks on
the faces of my congregation were rather discouraging."

Father Meyer realized at the outset that while many
Chinese, particularly children, were under-nourished the
same evil could befall foreigners as well. The Iowan was
apt to be quite stern about the missioners looking after
their own health. French padres had warned him that long
hours and improper food pretty soon crippled overzealous
newcomers and left them incapable of getting on with their
tasks. He was practical enough to understand why this was
so. It is his custom, to this day, when breaking in Maryknoll
fledglings in South China, to teach them how to care for
themselves physically. It has become Maryknoll legend that
Father Meyer's curates either take this advice, or pretty
soon cave in under the terrific work schedule he lays out
for them.

Most new missioners, and some veterans too, were apt to stand dismayed before new quarters in new territory, hopeless in the face of grime, disrepair and architectural faults and weaknesses. Father Meyer took these in full stride. To circumvent South China's white ants that hollow roof beams and flooring to paper thinness, he advocated impregnating construction beams with coal tar or creosote. The white ants backed away from the stuff and moved next door. Tropical damp ruined books, suitcases and trunks, but not Father Meyer's. He lacquered them with shellac to keep the damp out. Some missioners saw theirs accumulate mildew and rot.

He used a collapsible canvas bucket for hot foot baths on long mission treks over stony mountain roads. The Iowa plowman cooked hot soups on improvised stone stoves, with tomato cans for pots. When disinfectants were not handy, and often they were not, he'd make his own with ingredients from his medical kit or with chemicals acquired at the native shops. Nothing stumped him, not even music. When there's no one around to play the mission organ, he takes the console and his technique is satisfactory, if far from perfect.

Not an especially lightning-witted man, Father Meyer nevertheless showed the same flair for adaptation in social crises. This enabled him, many times, to squirm through situations that held embarrassing or face-losing possibilities and to lose face in China can delay a missioner's progress incredibly, particularly when he is trying to establish contact in high places. Early in his career at Wuchow Mission, Father Meyer was a dinner guest at the home of a

local patrician and it came time to go through the ceremonial rice wine drinking.

It is the custom for the host to hold the wine cup to the
guest's lips while the guest grasps the host's wrist with
the left hand. The process is reversed when the guest offers
the cup. As part of this Oriental rite, the host recites a
poetic Chinese toast. Then the guest, in turn, gets off an
appropriate poetic bauble. Father Meyer, as it happened,
wasn't up on the Chinese classics, but not to match the
host's eloquence would be to lose face. Father Meyer
proved equal to this situation, as to many others. Engaged
in the wine-drinking clinch he gravely recited the first
thing that came to mind. It was "Hi, diddle-diddle, the cat
and the fiddle, the cow jumped over the moon."

The host seemed delighted though Heaven knows what
he really thought. Anyway, the improvisation worked out
all right. The plowman, who's anything but a Merry
Andrew, never cracked a smile.

Courage is important in any missioner, but the Iowa
plowman had more than average courage. Two bus spills
on mountain paths that overhung deep gorges, encounters
with ubiquitous Chinese freebooters and mountain out-
laws didn't swerve him from his customary mission rounds.
Intermittent local wars bored him. In the Spring of 1920,
General Foo, a Kwangsi military gentleman of some im-
portance, took refuge in Father Meyer's compound in
Kochow and so did scores of frightened families. General
Wong, a Sun Yat Sen man from the neighboring province,
was right on General Foo's tail and hot for his prey.

General Foo, a discreet man, was outnumbered and in
no condition to take on General Wong. Before he dived

under a load of rice in Father Meyer's storage house, he begged Ma Shen Foo to talk things over for him with General Wong and to arrange a truce until around four o'clock in the afternoon, when he'd be ready to surrender. He made this plea at 10 o'clock in the morning. Father Meyer, who didn't want his parishioners hurt, rigged a flag of truce and mounted the compound's 20-foot wall. Wong's snipers, it turned out, were not familiar with truce flags. They wanged away at the Iowan but there were no hits. Father Meyer jumped back inside the wall.

Father Meyer got out a little American flag, crept along the parapet a second time and leaped for a stack of bamboo poles propped against the outside wall. He shinnied down and headed toward the invading party, waving the Stars and Stripes lustily. This got him through to General Wong. First of all, with characteristic Iowa directness, the missioner protested to the general against the attack on a compound filled with women and children. Then he submitted General Foo's truce plea. This seemed all right with General Wong. Father Meyer returned to the mission, dug into the rice, and broke the news to General Foo.

General Foo dusted off his uniform and seemed generally pretty well pleased with himself. "I've got Wong where I want him now," he confided slyly. "I expect re-inforcements around four o'clock. They'll take Wong's outfit from the rear." Such unethical conduct, even in a provincial war, was unusual. Father Meyer's anger exploded, but there was nothing much he could do. As it turned out, General Wong smelled a rat and attacked anyway. General Foo surrendered. To top things off, he decided to join up with Wong. What astonished the befuddled priests even more was the alacrity with which he was accepted. It seems Foo had, not without good basis for it, some reputation as a military strategist. Wong's side needed men like him.

These and similar incidents merely annoyed Father Meyer in his busy missionary career. He entered communities labelled "City of No Conversion." In many cases he gave the lie to the label. It wasn't as simple as it sounds. He often had to break down the local magistrate's opposition, then the elders' and last of all that of the general populace. Even in the most forbidding places, though, the old farm formula never let him down. He managed, somehow to turn the sod. Having turned it, he always planted the seed and stubbornly cultivated it until it flourished and grew strong and permanent roots. When the patch was easier to manage he'd turn it over to a new Maryknoll man and move on to the next field.

Yeungkong, Tungchen, Hoingan, Kochow, Pingnam— one by one they responded to the plowman's farmer philosophy and honest dealing. Maryknoll's field widened and expanded. His efforts for the poor were his best mediums of winning Chinese to Christianity. When floods receded, ruining the rice crop and poor folk's belongings, Father Meyer fed the unfortunate and provided seed with which, eventually, they could the more quickly feed themselves. He built schools, chapels, playgrounds, even out-door sun gardens, to cure ailing children. He was a human perpetual motion machine.

Between times he supervised his own kitchen, broke in and educated his own cooks—they were among the best in South China—sent for goats to provide milk for Chinese children who had never known this luxury. He kept pigs

and hens, and taught his houseboys a wealth of practical
little ways. He thought nothing of a forty-mile hike under
frying South China's Summer sun. A sick call, a wedding,
a baptism, brought him bolt upright from sleep, wide
awake and all set to move. A kit was always ready and
packed. Bewildered curates wilted at the mere thought of
this man's endless energy.

He was never self-indulgent. He looked constantly for
weaknesses and flaws in his own make-up and rooted them
out as any other farmer digs with the sharp end of his
hoe at crab grass. He was never careless about his dress,
because a shabby priest would lose face not only for himself but for his society.

Coolie porters with centuries of precedent to guide them
are pretty good, Father Meyer found, at arranging loads
in the baskets that dangle from either end of their shoulder
poles, but Father Meyer distributes his own mission kits
and other travelling equipment so the baskets balance to
a hair. At the same time, things are arranged in the order
in which they are to be used, which saves digging to the
bottom at each stop.

Coolies who snicker behind the good padre's back when
he steps briskly off on a long trek across mountain paths
made slippery by rains, pretty soon grow grim and then
panicky as he keeps it up, hour after tireless hour. They
have come to regard him with awe. "That Ma Shen Fu"
they say in the Chinese equivalent, when they're back with
their cronies, "don't ever try to outwalk that one." He
wades strong flowing currents, clambers over boulders, sets
a killing pace on the flat. He is conscious of the beauty of

country on his route, but doesn't waste time being romantic over it.

Only once—it was during his third year in China—did he seem to give in to nostalgia which is understandable in young missioners who find themselves 10,000 miles from home. He was pastor at Tungchen at the time and it was September. On a long trip into the mountains on a mission call a storm overtook him. He slipped off his shoes (he wears home-made cloth sandals because they're easier on the feet on mission circuits) and waded a swollen river. On the far bank, though, he didn't put the sandals on again.

"The feel of wet grass under my feet," he confessed in a letter to Maryknoll, "took me back fifteen years to when, on a rainy afternoon, I used to play through such grassy puddles as these, driving the cows home from pasture." Whether he recognized this as a momentary concession to nostalgia is any man's guess. In any case, nothing quite like it ever appeared again in his writing.

Father Meyer came back to the United States in 1926 on furlough, but not for vacation. He spent the months here travelling across the continent, lecturing on mission work and on the great need for expansion. The student body at St. Ambrose College in Davenport, his old school, raised enough funds for him to start a student's hostel in Pingnam. He came to the United States broken in health in 1936, but work was too much a habit with him to take it easy. He put in much time for China and the Chinese here. He hurried back eagerly to resume where he had left off, and has been at it with energy undiminished ever since.

Father Meyer, incidentally, is not the only member of his family with an astonishing capacity for work. Laboring in South China with him is his sister, Sister Mary Beatrice of the Maryknoll Sisters, who was Superior of the Maryknoll Convent at Yeungkong. She is broad, as he is, but darker. Her hands, through farm work as a girl, are broad. She has her brother's talent with tools, and nuns who have worked with her recall that she expertly repairs plumbing, executes professional bits of carpentry, handles livestock and displays green thumb in a vegetable or flower garden. She sews, is an excellent cook and faces dangerous moments with the same courage Father Meyer has always shown. "I'd say Sister Mary Beatrice can do just about everything, with one exception," one nun in the order has said. "She never writes poetry."

Father Meyer's courage under Japanese fire and his achievements in bringing civilians through the harrowing internment period at Hong Kong topped anything he had done previously, but that's a long story and will be told in another chapter. When Maryknoll men had a chance to get out of internment with other Americans to return to the United States, Father Meyer chose to stay on. He had made himself indispensable to the interned civilians and felt it was his duty to remain with them. When they pleaded that he needed the rest he quoted the words of Bishop James Anthony Walsh, Maryknoll's founder. "Better to wear out than rust out," he said, and turned back to his chores and his mission work.

Bishop Walsh, incidentally, summed up most missioners' attitude on this extraordinary man. When the Bishop heard about St. Ambrose College's gift for the Pingnam Hostel, he expressed gratitude for it. "I wish, though," he said wistfully, "that they'd send us more Father Meyers."

III

Father Sandy

AROUND ONE O'CLOCK on the morning of December 16, 1941, a sturdy little priest stood knee deep in restless surf off Sancian Island in the Pacific and strained against a Chinese sail boat to get it into deep water. Chinese boatmen, invisible in the black night, softly called their thanks as the vessel slid free. The boat's passengers—Mrs. Ch'ing and her children, Mrs. Lam and her brood, and two Maryknoll Sisters from the island convent—could not make out the figure in the tide. The nuns murmured, "God bless you, Father," but the message was smothered in surf crash.

How long Father Sandy stood there in the blackness with the sea swirling and sucking at his legs, the sail boat's passengers could not tell. Hours later, after dawn, they came ashore at Hoi Ngan, some fifteen miles across the strait. They had managed to slip past prowling Japanese warcraft in the pitch dark. After they had vanished, Father Sandy plodded up the firm beach to the little Maryknoll Mission. He was tired. Wading in the strong surf and straining at loaded boats tell quickly on a man just this side of sixty.

Father Robert J. Cairns—Sandy because he was Glasgow born, though bred in Worcester, Mass.—might have left Sancian on the boat, but he had lived a full decade on the island, guarding the spot where Saint Francis Xavier had died almost 400 years before and he chose to stay. Father John Joyce, his curate, was at Toi Shan, replacing a missioner who was ill in that post. But after years of solitude Father Cairns didn't mind that. "You are never lonely when you serve God," he used to say.

Seven hours after the boat had shoved off, Ching Wan Naam, the house-boy, entered the mission. He was excited. The Japanese had come again. He had seen them in a motor launch bristling with machine guns. They would be at the beach any moment. The missioner cautioned Ching to calmness. Soon afterward steps crunched on the gravel. In the doorway stood a Japanese officer. Behind him, rifles at ready, was a squad of his men.

Natives saw the Japanese lead the little priest to the beach, prod him into the boat and pull up anchor. The boat rounded a promontory and Father Cairns vanished from sight of those who had known him and loved him.

Maryknoll priests on the mainland heard numerous versions of what befell Father Cairns. Some of the Chinese on Sancian said the Japanese soldiers killed him and threw the body into the sea. When fishermen found a Panama hat drifting on the water near Wong King Chau Island, off Sancian, Ah Shui, the mission cook identified it. Other Chinese swore they saw the soldiers burn the priest's clothes and his religious books on the beach. A puppet soldier reported he had seen Father Cairns beheaded, the body thrown in the ocean.

Against this, mainland missioners got vague word that

the Japanese were holding Father Cairns on one of several islands, under internment as an American national—on Saam Tso To or on Tai Kam, a leper island. Nine months after Father Cairns was taken from the mission, word came through Switzerland to the American State Department in Washington that Father Cairns was a Japanese prisoner. The location of the prison was not given. Dead or alive, his house boy is with him. Ching had refused to leave him when the soldiers marched him down to the boat.

The little men from Japan had never scared the little man from Glasgow. For years he had done refugee work in much-bombed Canton. For months before they called for him that morning of December 16, he had remained among his parishioners on Sancian, calmly accepting the many hardships which the war had brought to his flock. The little men from Japan had burned every sampan and fishing junk they caught up with around the island, but Father Cairns and Father Joyce, his assistant, sailed the waters when their duty called for it. Over and over again they ran loads of rice in for the starving fishermen. Their boats were shot at by Japanese, but they got used to it.

Father Joyce, son of Hugh Joyce, a battalion chief in the New York City Fire Department, was alone one day in the Spring of 1941, when a Japanese destroyer put a group of soldiers ashore on Sancian. The naval officer who led the party wrote on a pad, in English, "We come to inspect." To the priest's astonishment, the officer removed his hat and bowed to the altar. He flipped through Father Joyce's breviary and other religious books. He wrote, "I have Bible too." He bowed to the padre and Father Joyce returned the bow.

"Hardly had I made my last bow," Father Joyce wrote home later, "when an irresponsible Murph (he always referred to the Japanese as Murphs, apparently out of Irish whimsicality) with fire in his eyes burst in on me. In one of the houses in San Tei Village on the island he had found a rifle and some bullets and the Chinese owner, unable to make clear that the gun was to protect his fields, brought the fellow to me. Whereupon, the Murph concluded that I was involved."

Father Joyce tried to make the Japanese understand, but the soldier all but burst with fury. Sancian Islanders had shot some twelve of his comrades when they had attempted a landing some weeks before. He thrust the rifle and bullets into the priest's face. "Kill" he exploded angrily, in English. "Kill."

"Accepting the inevitable," Father Joyce related in his account to Maryknoll, "I strode off about ten paces, turned and faced the fellow. I was determined he wouldn't see fear. He loaded the rifle, aimed and fired. He missed, of course, or I shouldn't be writing this, as the bullet merely moved my cassock sleeve. The brave lad turned on his heel and left the mission. I wasn't conscious of being particularly upset at the time, but was mortified later when I recalled that as a prayer of preparation for death I had recited, not the act of contrition but, of all things, grace before meals."

Father Joyce found it dangerous, sometimes, to attempt to put ashore on the mainland for rice, even after he had run the Japanese blockade and had tacked and run before Chinese pirates off Sancian. One Summer night, as he approached the mainland at Toi Shan, machine gun bullets and mortar shells screamed through his little ship's rigging. The mainlanders, it seems, were expecting a Japanese landing. "I'd stuck my chin out again," Father Joyce wrote home, resignedly. "For a half-hour it looked as though the pearly gates were open for me, but luckily I wasn't hit. I hustled farther up the coast and landed there."

Padre Joyce's fireman father likes to recall, now, what he said when his son first told him he was entering Maryknoll. "You're crazy, son," the Fire Chief told him. "Well, Dad," the boy answered, "If Saint Patrick had never come to Ireland as a missioner, you'd still be a heathen." "He had me there," the father concedes, but doesn't try to conceal family pride every time a Father Joyce exploit gets into the newspapers.

During 1940, when Father Cairns was laboring with the Red Cross at Shameen in Canton, Father Joyce was alone on Sancian. On January 21, 1941, he wrote: "Shipped 26,000 pounds of rice in six journeys with permission of the magistrate at Toi Shan. While there had to run a few times because of the birds. (Planes, he meant.) No damage." Other letters recorded how, "Burned boats float into Sancian with the tide, and sometimes goods. . . . . Last week eighteen boats were caught coming back from Hong Kong, right off the island. They were all burned and sunk. I took seven survivors to the mainland."

In September, 1941, Father Joyce visited Father Joseph Sweeney's leper colony at Gate of Heaven. "The last few weeks at the leper asylum were quite exciting," he wrote to his family. "Anything that moved was shot at from across the river. One leper was killed and a few refugees, too." The letter didn't mention that Father Joyce ran to the dying leper under Japanese fire, helped him to a sitting position and administered absolution just before the ma fung lo died. This information came from other sources, later. Like Father Cairns, young Joyce accepted the Japanese bombings as routine. On October 13, 1941, he wrote: "The Moifs are around quite some. Hope we don't meet any today, though. I'm leaving Toi Shan with another load of rice. We've had to row a lot. My hands have that old Pelham Bay look again."

Life on Sancian Island was no rosy dream, even before the Japanese swarmed down from Canton in the Fall of 1938. The island rises from warm seas off the southeast coast of China in toothy cliffs and crags some 120 miles south of Hong Kong. It is ten miles long and varies in width from three to five miles. Surf laps against, or charges onto the salty-white beaches according to the season, and sometimes the typhoon screams at them and piles the waves against the rocks in spume and fury.

It is a fishermen's paradise. Great schools of fish break water just off the beaches. Enormous dolphins sport in the ripples. When the tide is out, girls and women of Sancian wade bare-legged into the surf to knock mussels from exposed rock; gather sea weed for the pigs. There is little agricultural activity. In the valleys that lie between the mountains, a little rice is planted and a few industrious souls raise vegetables on terraced gardens, but mostly the men of Sancian—before the little men shelled and burned their picturesque craft—spread their nets in the sea and were assured of fish for their bowls, with some to spare for sale on the mainland.

There are no roads to speak of, and there is no radio, no telephone, no telegraph to keep Sancian in touch with the great world around it. The mainland is visible to the west on clear days, but when winds there are strong—as they often are—a sampan or a rowboat may take two nights and a day to negotiate the distance. The six thousand Chinese on the island live in tiny villages nestled in the valleys or clinging to hillsides. Conversion is difficult and only men like Father Sandy, with infinite patience and unwavering belief, could continue to shepherd a few souls at a time against heartbreaking odds.

On a peak at the western tip of Sancian, in 1552, Francisco de Xavier, only forty-six years old, but snowy-bearded and white-haired after superhuman achievements as a missioner, stared wistfully across the sparkling waters toward what he knew as the fabulous Middle Kingdom. His eyes and his cadaverous cheeks burned with fever, but at last he was within sight of the land to which he hoped to carry God's word to millions. No other missioner had penetrated so deeply into the Orient. Any hour, he thought, a Chinese boatman would carry him over the water from Sheung-chuen, as the Island was known then.

"God grant that he may not fail me," he wrote to the Rev. Francis Perez, S.J., on October 22, 1552, but the boatman never came. Francisco de Xavier died a few weeks later. The last image in his fading sight was the mainland of the Middle Kingdom. A solid little Gothic chapel marks the spot, now. The windows were broken when Father Cairns came to the island ten years ago. He replaced them with brick, cleared out the floors where water buffalo and cows had wandered, and tenderly cleaned the tombstone

that marks the spot where the Saint's body rested until it
was removed to Goa.

"It is a duty and privilege to be custodian of the church
enclosing this tomb," he often said to visitors. "From this
island, where he lived and died, I try to make Xavier
better known and loved."

The mission rectory lies around a bend in the beach,
a half-hour's· walk or so from the tomb. From this spot,
Father Cairns journeyed to remote places on the island,
smilingly inviting Christians and pagans alike to his service. The little man in the silver-rimmed spectacles—and,
incidentally, he liked to recall that Saint Xavier was only
five feet, one inch in height—was familiar to the fisher
folk. Even non-Christians responded to his smile. Some
days, when his feet were sore, he'd walk in the dusty valleys
and across the cruel mountain paths, barefoot like the
monks of medieval time, but even unshod he was a dignified
figure that commanded respect.

A full month before Easter Father Cairns would lay in
a supply of holiday foods and, according to Chinese custom, would send invitations to families in the Sancian villages to be his guests at the service and at the feast. In
Sancian, as on the mainland though, it is polite to send
three invitations to each prospective guest. Father Cairns'
house boy would carry one to the village elders, then his
cowherd would carry another and, finally, Father Sandy
would sally out on foot and bring the last one himself.

Usually rains fell gently as he clambered over slippery
mountain paths, or hopped from one jagged boulder to
another, on this errand. One minute he was knee deep in
a gully with the tepid water reaching for his uplifted cas-

sock, a few minutes later flood waters tore at his bare feet on a rude little bridge. At *Sha Peng*, or the Village Sandy Plains, one of the first stops, he would sit gravely with the wrinkled elders and talk, with the indirection he had learned from the Chinese, of crops and children and the fishing. The rain dripped from his cassock and formed fat puddles on the mud floor. The bamboo pipe of friendship was passed from one withered hand to another. The invitation, on the red paper the Chinese love, would at long last be presented, with two hands—this is the rigid custom—to the presiding elder, who would accept it with his two hands. The elders would bow the little padre to the door and he would return the bow, the light picking glints from his spectacles, and move off in the rain again. It would be the same at Mudfish Village, at North Hollow, High Crown, Sandy Pool and Bamboo Stone, at Fresh Fish Plain and Cheen Family Village and at Stand On Your Head In the Sand. The trip would cover 26 to 30 difficult miles.

On Sunday morning the Easter guests would trudge down the mountains and through the valleys before the sun was in the sky. The little church would be rich with paper streamers, the saw-horse pews were scrubbed and sunned and the altar, washed with oil, gave back the sun's light. The church was cool and communicants, adrip with perspiration after the long hike, were grateful. Four white-clad barefoot Chinese altar boys led the procession from sacristy to altar and the air grew sweet with chanted hymns. Father Cairns read the Gospel from Chinese characters.

The women sat at the back of the Church. Mothers untied the cloth lengths that bound their children to their backs and turned the infants loose, like so many puppies, on the Church floor. "The little ones are a distraction to Western ears," Father Cairns often explained, "but the Chinese have always had it so and if the children's cries do not disturb them at their devotions, certainly I do not mind." After Benediction, the guests would sit in groups of ten on the grass for the feast; the air would fill with shrill chatter and Father Cairns would look benignly on the play of chopsticks in the rice bowls.

Before sundown the guests would sing-song their polite and grandiloquent farewells to Father Cairns and start home again along mountain and valley trails. He would stand, watching the departure into the setting sun until the last had vanished from his sight. "Blessed be God," he'd murmur. Wearily, then, he'd get on with the few remaining duties and offices, climb into bed, usually with a detective novel in his hands and read till the volume was released from his fingers by sleep induced by whispering surf.

Father Cairns was fond of telling about his first Midnight Mass on Sancian in 1933. At daybreak on Christmas Eve he trudged over the hills to *Sai Ngau Peng* and preached a Christmas sermon to some fifty Chinese, moved on to the next village and repeated the service. Around eleven o'clock that night he walked from the mission, around the bend to the tomb chapel. His lantern shed white circles on the white beach sand, on the gray rock as he climbed the hill to the peak.

"There were only a few who dared climb that path in midnight's inky blackness," he'd relate, "even to hear the Mass at the sacred shrine. There were eleven, all told. Suddenly, the bell in the tower announced to Sancian

Island the coming of Christ. It was the first time that a tower bell had rung there for many years. I don't know for how long. A few months before we had rebuilt the tower; I had brought the bell back from *Taai Long Waan* (Harbor of Great Waves) whither mischievous hands had removed it. The sound of that bell at Midnight thrilled me to the heart.

"I stood by the empty tomb, read the Gospel of the first Christmas Mass and I felt, somehow, that Xavier stood there with me. I told the story of the birth of Jesus. 'Here, on this spot' I told my parishioners, 'three hundred and eighty years ago, lay the body of St. Francis Xavier, covered with lime in its wooden coffin, the body incorrupt, as it remains today at Goa in India. Millions of Catholics in the world envy us our privilege of hearing Midnight Mass in this hallowed shrine.'"

One among the worshippers at the tomb that night was a blind Chinese woman. Her face was withered and scored with etched shadow by the candlelight, but her expression was beatific. Tears welled in Father Cairns' eyes and sparkled behind the silver-rimmed glasses. "I read the Gospel to this one blind woman, and preached to her alone," he said. "I thought, this one confession of a blind woman of strong faith is beyond computing. I thought, four thousand Sancian Islanders have eyes and see not; she has no sight, but sees deeply with the eyes of faith."

In 1934, Father Sandy had a motor launch that gave him sure and easy access to the mainland. It was The Crusader, a gift from Monsignor Frank Thill, director of the Catholic Students' Mission Crusade, now Bishop Thill of Concordia, Kansas. Ah Lam, a mission house-boy who knew all about junks and sampans, but not much about motor launches, went into the boathouse one night with a match and inadvertently touched off the gasoline. Ah Lam leaped into the sea, aflame. Moxie, a catechist, O. K., the cook and Chop Suey, a house boy, stood with Father Sandy and fought the fire with quilts and blankets soaked in sea water. "There's something attractive about a fire reflected on waves at night," the padre confided afterward, "and from early childhood in Worcester I'd always liked to run to fires, but that night the spectacle was not fascinating." The Crusader was irreparably damaged.

When other Maryknollers came to Sancian, the island padre would plead with them to sing. His boyhood home in Worcester, filled with ten Cairnses, always rang with cheery song, and sometimes he missed the solace and comfort of old melodies. On Sancian he had a few scratchy, ancient recordings—"The Market on Saturday Night," the Lauder numbers, "Two Little Girls in Blue," and "Maggie Murphy's Home."

Father Patrick H. Cleary of Ithaca, N. Y., a Korean Maryknoller, recalls one midnight when he and Father Cairns were in a sampan off Sancian and they sang, probably to the startled astonishment of nearby Chinese, "We're All Toddlin' Down the Brae."

"It was after our boatmen had gone to sleep," Father Cleary remembered, "and after we had said our rosary together. The South China Sea, so close you could touch it with your hand, was alive with phosphorescence. Father Sandy said the song made him think of his mother. He said she couldn't read a note, but she'd sing all day at home in Worcester, mostly Irish and Scottish melodies, and "We're

Toddlin' Down The Brae," was one of her favorites. He said 'What's a mere ten thousand miles between Mother and me?' but his eyes swam with tears."

Sometimes before breakfast, often in the dead of night Sancian Catholics would call Father Cairns over the mountains, or into the valleys to administer last rites to the dying. He always went, without murmur. Rosary, meditation, Mass, Breviary took a good two hours out of each day. In between, he was judge, and sometimes one-man jury, in an extraordinary range of village disputes and litigation.

An excitable group from Stand On Your Head In The Sand, one day, even wanted Father Cairns to act as detective. "Will the Shen Fu—Spiritual Father—" they wanted to know, "discover who stole the cow whose bones, stripped of all meat, were left in front of the Young Men's Meeting Place?" Would the Good Father, through his power of persuasion, extract from the thief (whoever he might be) the round basket, half-filled with bees and honey, that was stolen from the Wongs while they slept last night? Will Father contribute a generous donation for a new bridge at Great Hollow, since he is compelled to wade through the mud to get to the village? Another duty, in which he never failed, was the dispensing of medicines to the sick. This took a few hours each day.

Yet, life among the fisher folk was comparatively easy, from the missioners' viewpoint, until the Japanese came down from Canton. Thirty Sancian dwellers lay hidden among the cliffs when the first Japanese launch charged through the surf. The defenders' weapons were primitive but their fire dropped a score of the invaders and drove the others back to their boats. Next morning—it was in October—Sancian rocked and shuddered as aerial bombs thudded on helpless villages. The fisher folk ran for their ancient craft with their belongings on their backs and their children queued out behind them.

The Japanese landed that day, set fire to the few wretched shops, burned some of the dwellings. Then, for no apparent reason, they withdrew.

Hundreds of Sancian natives including many who had never been off the island, crossed in their boats to the mainland, where they mingled with other refugees who swarmed mainland highways. Some came back when the Japanese left, but these later lost their boats to the enemy and were starved until Father Cairns ran rice from Toi Shan. One afternoon a group of pagan boys came to the mission from the eastern tip of Sancian. They had never wandered so far from home before, but they were hungry. Before Father Cairns could feed them a Japanese destroyer loomed on the horizon. The children fled in fear, presumably to trek the 15 miles homeward, though they were mere bags of bones from starvation.

Whenever Japanese bomber pilots soared above Sancian, they created terror among the villagers with their explosives, and vanished again. On December 9, 1941, at one o'clock in the afternoon Japanese soldiers and a puppet troop landed on the island. Father Cairns saw they were headed for the little convent. He held them a while with earnest pleading, but eventually they broke into the convent and looted it clean. Father Cairns' intervention gave the nuns and their charges time to flee into the hills.

Three days before he was taken from the island, Father

Cairns had a Japanese visitor, a rather polite officer. He advised the little padre to leave for the mainland, even offered passage in his launch. Father Cairns, matching his visitor's politeness, quietly elected to stay. The Japanese officer said, "Your country and my country are at war." This was news to Father Cairns. He had no contact with the outside world, not even a radio. The officer said, "Our planes have smashed your Pearl Harbor and Honolulu. We have taken Hong Kong." Father Cairns clung to his decision.

"I can save you, if you leave with me now," the officer told him. "Tomorrow Japanese from other places may come. They will come to kill."

He left the island without Father Cairns. That night, though, Father Cairns went into the hills. He arranged for the passage of the two Maryknoll Sisters. He told them he knew his duty was on Sancian. He would not go with them. Two nights later he shoved their boat into the black tide.

Four months after Father Cairns and the faithful Ching Naam disappeared around the peak, beneath St. Xavier's shrine, starving Sancian Islanders raided the little mission —then a Japanese warehouse—and looted it clean of flour, sugar, kerosene and most of the mission property. They shot down the three Japanese who were on the island. Chinese puppet soldiers, oddly enough, helped them. One Japanese ran to the sacristy of Father Cairns' little church, opened four tins of kerosene and tried to burn himself to death. A puppet's bullet ended his writhings. A few days later ten boat loads of Japanese came ashore. The natives fled to the hills and looked down helplessly as the little men set fire to their homes.

On June 12, Father James Smith of Maryknoll heard that the Japanese had deserted Sancian. On July 12, a Japanese destroyer stood off shore and destroyed the convent, the rectory, and left only the church walls standing. Shall these ruins beckon back at war's end the little padre of Scotch cheer? God alone can give us a trustworthy answer.

IV

Bombs and Bayonets

THE CHINA CLIPPER roared past native swimmers who had cleared its track of floating logs in Cavite Harbor at daybreak, December 7, 1941, buried its nose to the portholes in spume, then shook itself free with a tremendous shudder. Six hours later eight new Maryknoll men, fresh from the States, saw Hong Kong beneath them sunning in the sea. Wavelets slapped and sucked at the Clipper's hull as it took them to the landing at Kai Tak air base and set them ashore.

Maryknoll's Hong Kong house celebrated Father Meyer's twenty-fifth ordination anniversary that night. The new men listened to yarns of the missions and answered hundreds of questions about home and home folk. Lights burned late on this special occasion but neither newcomers nor veterans realized that those were to be the last bright lights they'd see in Hong Kong, that the anniversary dinner was to be their last full meal for a long time.

There was a double shock at breakfast next morning. One of the missioners walked in as the new men sipped their coffee. "The Japanese have bombed Pearl Harbor," he said tensely. "It's on the radio." Missioners started from their chairs, staring into each other's faces. Nobody said much. Before they left the dining room, Maryknoll House bounced and trembled. The Japanese were over Kai Tak. They had shattered the China Clipper, and were bombing the island.

Father Meyer was the first to come out of the daze. He pointed out with characteristic foresight that in Hong Kong under siege, food would become scarce and more expensive. He arranged for future supplies and sent Chinese boys into town to fetch them. The mission went on shore rations immediately—rice, beans, occasional meats and vegetables. Father Meyer supervised blackouts for the windows. Hong Kong grew shrill with terror as whites and Chinese fled for the dugouts. Bombs shook the city without let-up. Missioners clustered around the radio. They could still get San Francisco but what they heard only further sickened them. "It seemed fantastic," Father Michael McKeirnan recalled later. He was from Pomeroy, Washington, one of the eight youngsters who had come in on the Clipper less than twenty-four hours before. "The plane that had landed us was already blown to bits. There was laughter and happiness at the anniversary dinner. Now we grouped around the radio like vultures."

Father Meyer and Father John Toomey, Superior for Maryknoll in Hong Kong, worked out an emergency schedule. There were no deviations from religious routine. The eight newcomers were sent into Hong Kong to register with the British, but never reached the registry office. In the Aberdeen district they leaped from their bus, along with Chinese passengers, and bounded for the air-raid shelters. The ground rocked and danced under bomb impact.

The shelters were low, winding caves. The lighting was dim and men and women trod on one another's feet. Children whimpered or shrieked in terror. Chinese gabbled excitedly. The ventilation was poor and the caves grew stuffy. After a long time the earth-shaking stopped, a siren called all-clear and the men climbed into daylight again. There were no British planes in the sky. The Zeros and Japanese bombers had the air to themselves and left it only to fly back to the mainland to reload their bomb racks.

The bus took the riders on less than a mile before bombs thudded into earth again. The Maryknoll men ducked into a gully. They saw the enemy planes glinting in the sun, watched with breathless fascination as the bombs plummeted and instinctively shut their eyes at the explosions. Down by the ferry, a few hundred yards from the gully, bombs created great water geysers. Heavy black smoke rolled from burning homes and stores on Stonecutters' Island. The smoke was shot with hot flame.

One air alarm followed the other and Father Toomey decided it would be best to leave registration for another day. A returning bus rumbled to a stop nearby but it was already crowded and Chinese and white civilians fought for space enough to put one foot and to get an armhold. The men had barely established such precarious holds before another bomber formation sailed overhead, a cross formation, twelve planes each way. There was another breathless scramble for the caves, another waiting period until the earth stopped shuddering.

The alarm wailed and echoed once more against Hong Kong's granite heights when the young missioners and all other passengers had weighted the bus so the spring leaves

lay flat, but this time only a few released their fingertip
grips to run for the caves. The harried bus driver got the
vehicle into groaning motion. Twilight had come. Flame
and smoke seemed to rim the whole island. A British guard
stopped the bus. Father Toomey and the new men, a few
nuns and a group of Chinese started afoot for Stanley
where the dark was closing down.

The group came to a startled halt as rifle fire cracked
out somewhere ahead and bullets pinged and whistled in
close passage. Father Toomey stared into the gloom and
made out a British Tommy, rifle at firing position. "Ahoy
there," he called. "What's wrong with you? We're Americans from Stanley." The Tommy recognized the accent. He
called back, "You didn't heed my challenge, man. Come
ahead, single file." The new men, the nuns and Father
Toomey moved up one by one, for identification. The little
group of Chinese had either misunderstood, or failed to
hear the challenge. One lay dead in the path.

The Maryknoll party moved on, calling out hoarsely at
frequent intervals in the darkness to warn other British
sentries and patrols of their approach. The sky was pat-
terned with tracer bullets, red and white. British ack-ack
guns coughed and barked on the outer rim of Hong Kong.
In some quarters of the city whole blocks were aflame. The
registration party pushed through the house door exhausted. It was 10 P. M. Since the anniversary party at
the same hour the night before, the world had gone mad.

The group that had gone to the city found the house
aswarm. British Royal Engineers had commandeered one
of the floors. Fifty of their coolies were digging entrench-
ments around the building. Lieutenant Lawrence, the tall

blond British officer in charge wanted the whole building but Father Meyer had talked him out of it. The officer had arranged to shelter the Maryknoll men in another house in Stanley Village, but Father Meyer explained he had no way to move all the Maryknoll stores and equipment. It was just as well that the Iowa plowman held out on this point. The house in the village was flattened to the earth by Japanese bombs on Christmas Day.

Lieutenant Lawrence's men took over the priests' recreation room on the second floor. Father Meyer set up new recreation space in the auxiliary chapel. The priests sat round, smoking more than was good for them, but after a while tension seemed to ease, though bombs still fell and ack-ack rained from the sky. Around midnight a British officer from Stanley Fort stamped into the house. He insisted lights could be seen in it from the post. Father Meyer, who had made the blackout curtains light-proof, challenged this statement. It turned out the lights were on the upper floor where the Royal Engineers were quartered. The officer apologized.

From their windows on the hill the Maryknoll staff saw Japanese bombs hit all around them. Sometimes Zeros pivoted around their roof, flying low, so that a projecting wing seemed to all but come through the pane. From Stanley Fort the heavy British 9.2 cannon boomed almost constantly. At night the missioners saw the brief angry red flash as it spat and the explosion shook the house and set up rumbling echoes. They were firing at enemy craft off Kowloon, across the bay. When the British called for volunteers to dig more shelters, the priests pitched in. They worked beside a chain gang from Stanley Prison. Word came, at this time, that the Japanese had taken Kowloon.

British, Canadian and Indian soldiers flowed in and out of Maryknoll House. They looked worn and grimy, but they did not complain. They exchanged some of their cold rations, sometimes, for a hot plate of soup, too busy to cook their own. One night the whole island rocked as under a mighty earthquake. The dynamite cache at Stonecutter's Island had been hit. All that night the sky was rimmed with high-leaping flame as if the world were afire. One of the priests said, "It seems like an evil red omen."

Father Meyer sternly kept the new men at their language study. He paced nervously up and down. He chanted, "ah, ah, ah, ah," teaching the Cantonese dialect, and the new men repeated the chant. One afternoon a stray bullet pinged through the classroom window, ricocheted off the wall. Glass splinters flicked Father Meyer's right cheek. He quietly applied a handkerchief to the wound—it was slight—but, never lost stride or dropped a syllable. "Ah, ah, ah," he intoned, and went on to the next note. It had a steadying effect on the class.

The invading Japanese crept closer to Maryknoll House each passing day. It turned out that for more than two years they had prepared for this attack. Through intermediaries they had bought certain old warehouses in Kowloon and inside the warehouses they had set up heavy concrete gun emplacements. When they were ready to take Hong Kong they hacked away the fronts of these buildings and British observers were startled to see heavy artillery revealed, snugly bedded down in the concrete gun positions so cunningly concealed. These cannon put the fort under heavy bombardment.

The missioners were spectators watching a grim show. From their windows they saw men, horribly wounded crawl away to die. They saw peaceful green lawn blossom in thunderous flame and smoke, into sudden deep craters. They saw Father Toomey, morning after morning, walk placidly along shelled roads toward the British hospital to give spiritual comfort to British wounded. Late in the afternoon they would see him again, a small, gentle man, gravely plodding homeward against a backdrop of bursting shells and heaving earth. One afternoon as he kneeled beside a wounded Canadian in the road, a shell thudded close and sprayed them with hot debris. Father Toomey dragged the Canadian under a truck for shelter and got on with his office.

In the second week of the siege, the Japanese sent over night landing parties. British mortars and machine guns tore these parties to shreds. In the city of Hong Kong, Japanese fifth-columnists were at work. Word drifted back to Maryknoll House that British troop trucks and supply vans were blown up by grenades dropped from rooftops at night as they moved from one harassed position to another. Later, when the Japanese landed, cooperators rolled trucks to the beach to pick up invading battalions. The plan had obviously been a long time in preparation.

Father Meyer piled furniture and loaded book cases against the windows and doors for added protection against rifle and machine gun fire as the Japanese moved steadily inland from their beach-heads. By the middle of December, the missioners were quite accustomed to the ping and screech of stray bullets. These flattened against the wall brick, shattered windows and bit wood from window frames. The invaders took Wang Nei Chung Gap after bitter hand-to-hand fighting and pressed the defenders back. They took Tytam reservoir, and Maryknoll House, along with the whole of Hong Kong, was cut off from its main water supply.

The nights were difficult. With water rationed, the situation was even more tense. The only available light now came from feeble oil lanterns and from vigil candles. Reading was difficult. The missioners and the wounded soldiers sat in semi-darkness and talked of home. The soldiers showed pictures of their wives and children, spoke wistfully of remembered hearty steak dinners and cold beer. Wounded men were carried in constantly and the priests tended their wounds and gave them religious comfort. The meagre supply of water left in house tanks and boilers was shared with these unfortunates.

Maryknoll House eventually stood directly in the line of fire between the British Fort and the hills occupied by the invaders. Shells screamed over the roof in both directions. After dark, the missioners saw the skies about them hemstitched with red and white tracers, like a gigantic peasant kerchief. Bullets now beat unceasing bastinado on the house walls and whistled steadily through the windows, especially on the upper floors. Day and night the missioners were hemmed in the lower corridors. Their altars were set up there. They ate and slept there. Father Meyer had them stack sacks of rice and dried prunes against the most exposed spots, to absorb bullets.

On the morning of December 23, the Japanese occupied rising ground within sight of Maryknoll House. They sprayed a knot of coolies on the lawn with machine gun

fire. The priests rushed out, dragged the wounded indoors
and applied first aid. The coolies' cries and moans as anti-
septic touched their hurts, filtered through rooms and corridors. There was little, or no sleep in the house that night.
Gunfire was deafening. The building literally rocked under
it. The missioners saw a shell tear open part of St. Stephen's
Episcopal College between their place and the fort. Another
shell collapsed a house near the college. "The British soldiers are crawling out of the debris like ants" one of the
new missioners murmured. "They must be badly hurt."

On December 24, the missioners took care of the
wounded, attended to religious duties and in odd moments
resignedly sat down to play at cards. They had become
more or less accustomed to the house's rocking under cross-
fire. A Canadian crawled along the lawn, toward sundown,
banged at the door and begged for some of the hot beans
that were on the oil stove. "We're fixing a kind of Christmas Eve dinner, Father," he told Father Meyer. "We're
off there in the woods, holding the Japs off, but we thought
a hot snack for Christmas . . ." Father Meyer filled the
soldier's dish with a generous helping. The missioners,
through cracks in the curtains, watched the Canadian crawl
back toward the woods under intense fire. He made it somehow. They prayed for him every inch of the way.

That night, as Father McKeirnan whimsically recalls it,
was like "Night on Bald Mountain" in the Disney fantasy.
The Heavens split with thunderous artillery flashes. Guns
of every size and calibre made hideous din. Death screamed
from all sides and from the sky. The tracers seamed night's
blackness in a variety of luminous threads. Flares soared
over Stanley Fort and their ghastly light shed spectral glow

over great areas of rock and hillside. Gigantic blocks of
shadow it created seemed to crouch and leap. Worst of all
were the screams and cries of wounded, calling out of the
night. The missioners slept in the house corridors that
Christmas Eve with the two floors in a constant jig.

On Christmas morning, the missioners stirred from their
mattresses, tidied the corridors and celebrated Mass. The
Japanese were shrill on the hillside, close enough now so
that their high-pitched voices were audible between bursts
of fire. At seven o'clock, while some of the men were still
at devotions, gun butts shattered what remained of the
glass panels in the doors and a Japanese chorus shouted
angry demands for entry. Father Meyer, finished at the
altar, clumped downstairs. He dragged bags of rice and
prunes from the barricades. As the door swung back four
little men with green branches fixed in the netting on their
helmets, jabbed bayonets against his cassock and showed
their teeth.

"Kill," they snarled. "We kill." Father Meyer didn't
back up, as they apparently intended he should. They were
astonished at the Iowan's seeming indifference to their
threats, and somewhat admired it. In rapid Cantonese,
which they seemed to grasp, he explained that this was a
house for missioners, for men of the church. They discussed
this among themselves for a moment, thrust Father Meyer
aside, and entered. Some forty to fifty piled into the house
with bayonets at the ready, the green leaves on their helmets
quaking grotesquely as they moved. Each time they encountered another missioner they lunged at him, but in each
case withheld the death thrust. They accompanied these
lunges with fierce grunts. They shouted to one another and

the building was noisy with their cries as they scattered through the rooms and up the stairs.

The Japanese herded the missioners into the big front room and commanded them to sit on the tiled floor. Guards were set over the prisoners, dark-faced little men who seemed to enjoy hissing—at the captives. Some of the soldiers came down the stairs and from the kitchen, their arms filled with canned goods. They jabbed holes in the cans with their bayonets and sampled their loot. What they liked they gulped in great quantities. They guzzled tomato juice and didn't seem to mind when it flowed too fast and coursed down their chins and tunics.

They burst open cans of fruits and meat. What they did not consume they threw to the tiles and the mess soon attracted swarms of flies. They poked greedily in bags and closets and compared their prizes in cameras, watches, clocks and fountain pens, wallets and cigarette lighters. One lugged in a full case of ginger ale he had found in the store room. He set it on the floor, picked up a bottle and got at the contents by biting off the top with his broad teeth. They broke open cartons of American cigarettes and jammed their pockets full.

Father Meyer, miraculously, moved among them as if they were neighbors from next door. A Japanese soldier who had found a pistol in one of the rooms, fired into the front room wall, over the heads of a group of trembling coolies and Chinese house-boys who were seated on the floor. Father Meyer stared coldly at the soldier, and the Jap pocketed the weapon. The Iowan went downstairs to the cellar to see to the Mass wine. He discovered in the supply a number of bottles, poorly corked, that had turned to

vinegar. These he lined up in the first two rows. It was a
wise move. A Japanese officer and a little cluster of his
aides, searching the house a few minutes later, entered the
cellar and sampled the front-row wine. They spat it out,
tried the second row and again registered distaste. The
good Mass wine in the back was never touched. Upstairs,
meanwhile, Japanese soldiers snatched wrist watches from
missioners' wrists and lifted pens from their jackets.

Several wounded Japanese were carried in and were laid
on the floor. The sight of their own wounded seemed to
enrage the guards. One of them snarled at Father Meyer,
accused him of helping the English and telling lies. The
Iowa priest answered in even tones. It was no fault of the
missioners, he told the guard, that British soldiers had
commandeered the house. "They are soldiers, we are men
of the church," he told the heavily-breathing Japanese. The
missioners, helpless on the floor, held their breath throughout this argument, but again Father Meyer's bold front
prevailed. The guard turned away.

Savage outcry at the door turned the missioners' heads
suddenly in that direction. A squad of Japanese had Lieutenant Lawrence. He towered over them like Gulliver in
Lilliput. One Japanese soldier got up on tip toe and slapped
the lieutenant's face so the smack resounded. Lieutenant
Lawrence, bound, simply stared at the man. His lips tightened. Other Japanese ripped the buttons and epaulets from
his tunic. Several spat in his face. One of his tormentors
jabbed a pistol into the lieutenant's chest and exploded in
his native tongue. The lieutenant heard him out in stony
silence. Neither he nor the watching circle understood a

syllable of it but took it for what it probably was, a charging torrent of hatred and invective.

Some of the missioners nearest the canned goods spilled on the tile, picked up a few cherries, peaches and tuna fish, some of it covered with cigarette ashes. Father Leonard Madison of Syracuse, N. Y., one of the new men, edged toward the store room and got his hand into a cookie jar. A Japanese guard caught him at it, backed away and kicked him savagely. This was the Christmas dinner. In the same moment, Father Murphy, a Canadian missioner from Chekiang in Hong Kong for medical treatment, bent over to help a wounded British soldier. The motion disclosed khaki trousers under the cassock.

Hell broke loose. A Japanese soldier tore at the cassock, ripped it and screamed to attract his fellows' attention. What he was saying, it turned out, was that all the priests were British soldiers disguised as missioners. Glaring Japanese plunged among the Maryknoll men. Their invective touched a new, shrill high. They forced the missioners to kneel and bound them with rope in little knots of four and five, each with his wrists behind his back. Lieutenant Lawrence had been tied so that his least movement tightened a noose around his neck. One end of the noose rope was tied to his wrists. His face got red, then purple. The Japanese seemed to enjoy this. Father Meyer, lips pursed, strode across the room and undid the noose. Several soldiers leaped for him, but an officer sharply called them off.

The missionaries were on the tile from eight o'clock in the morning until almost four o'clock that Christmas Day. The bonds were irksome, at first, then increasingly painful. They bit into the wrists and any one man's move meant suffering for the others in his group. The prisoners heard the Japanese moving through the house, smashing doors with their rifle butts, shattering glass panes.

Just before 5 o'clock the British officers and soldiers in the house were prodded to their feet and were led outdoors. At 5 P.M., a Japanese officer commanded the missioners to rise, which they managed with difficulty. They were grateful, though, for the chance to get to standing position. Their limbs were cramped and their arms were numb. This time, Father Meyer was bound with all the rest. They were marched to the door over the debris and the precious canned foods spilled on the tile, guards prodding them with bayonets as they passed. They were led down the driveway and down the hill along an unused side road. A silver plane swooped toward them. The Japanese scurried for the ditches and the priests stumbled out of the road with them. The captives could not identify the plane. It did not open fire.

A little distance farther on, the road passed between high embankments. The missioners were shoved down to sitting positions under one bank. Over their heads machine gun bullets whined and British shells whistled, screamed, and burst among creeping invaders. Japanese fire whanged and moaned from the opposite direction. A Japanese officer called a sharp command to his men and the British prisoners, Lieutenant Lawrence, four of his Royal Engineers and two Canadian soldiers, were hauled to their feet.

The British prisoners were marched around a bend in the road. A few minutes later cries of extreme agony made the missioners squirm. The Japanese were putting the bound soldiers to the bayonet. Orders at this juncture in the hideous island fight were to take no prisoners; this little group was obeying to the letter. The screams lasted hardly more than two minutes. One Canadian enlisted man broke past the end of the gauntlet and the missioners stared in horrified fascination as several little men thrust savagely at him till he stopped writhing. The chattering attackers, eyes aflame with battle lust, approached the missioners, wiping the blood from their bayonets as they walked.

Brother Thaddeus of Oberlin, Ohio, of the Maryknoll Hong Kong staff understood Japanese. He murmured, "They're arguing about us. They're saying we're soldiers in disguise. They're for doing us in." The missioners heard this in silence.

The officer went down the line, cross-examining the bound men in poor English. He tried to trap them, examined their secondary garments for military markings, but, of course, found none. At the end of the embankment, in the road, a Japanese non-com talked into a portable microphone. The transmitter-receiver was hitched to his back, pack fashion. He made notes on a little pad. One of these notes he tore off and handed to the officer. The officer studied it, glanced quizzically into the faces up and down the prisoners' line. He barked an order and the priests were prodded to their feet.

The missioners, by this time, were resigned to death. They had seen with their own eyes the ruthlessness that battle can bring and they had no hope for themselves. They had given each other absolution, and every man among them was prepared. Talking about this moment, later, the men remembered the quick series of thoughts that flashed through their minds—mental pictures of home, of the seminary at Maryknoll in New York, of mothers, brothers and sisters. They murmured farewells to one another, and tried to get a note of cheer into the words. Another rasping command started them moving, bayonets at their ribs or rumps, toward the break in the road where Lieutenant Lawrence and his men had died. "Here we go, boys," someone called out. A Japanese guard hit him with the flat end of a bayonet. The priests cast one glance at the pitiful, distorted bodies that had been British soldiers, but hastily looked away again.

To the missioners' astonishment, the column did not turn down the narrow gulch where the Britons had died. The Japanese guide tramped past it in the descending twilight. A sigh, almost audible, escaped the prisoners' lips. They expected death, but at least it was not to be at this spot. They did not realize it immediately, but by a miracle of temperateness on the part of the Japanese command, the instruction on the field telephone had decreed life to the men of the church. The file tramped to the foot of the hill, to a garage behind a Chinese house, still within sight of their home quarters. A Japanese soldier opened the garage door and the priests were shoved over the threshold. In semi-darkness they stumbled over old flower pots, and heaps of dirty rags and barked their shins against sharp metal projections standing knee high in the gloom. These were the metal ends of damaged cots, they learned later.

On command, the missioners—there were thirty-five, including Bishop O'Gara of the Passionists and other non-Maryknollers,—were disposed on the damp garage floor. Baby chicks peeped hysterically between their feet. They could hear the chicks, but it was growing too dark to see them. Their own faces, closely bound though they were, showed up as vague white patches. Some of the men tried to arrange themselves to lie down, but this was impossible except in a few cases because of the tight bonds. Where one man put a strain on the rope, the strands cut more deeply into the wrists of the others. There was another reason for remaining fixed. Each time a group milled for better position, some metal or earthenware object fell or crashed and Japanese guards threw the door open, charging with bayonets set to thrust. It was not a merry Christmas.

A half-hour after the men had been herded into the garage, a Japanese opened the door and with bayonet held forward, moved among the missioners. A non-com behind him with flashlight and drawn pistol searched the upturned faces. He picked Father Madison, Father John P. Tackney of Somerville, Mass., and Father Wence F. Knotek of Racine, Wis., three of the eight youngsters who had come in on the Clipper. They were ordered to stand. Knots were retied in the groups from which they were taken, and the Japanese herded them toward the door. Madison—he was "Tarzan" at the seminary—called good-bye as he passed. The garage door closed on the murmured prayers of the men who were left behind. They did not pray for themselves.

Gunfire and machine gun bursts still whistled, pinged and roared, each according to its habit, and the garage floor trembled as Maryknoll House had trembled. The men sitting in the dark garage strained their ears for rifle shots, and for possible cries of agony—they were certain the younger men were merely the first three chosen for slaughter—but they heard only the shrill Japanese and a constant shuffle and pounding of feet. Ten minutes later the garage door creaked open again and the three young priests were back among them. The Japanese had wanted them to fill sandbags for a machine-gun emplacement, but British fire had found the spot and the Japanese had changed their minds.

Around seven o'clock that night, the area suddenly grew quiet. Barrage fire died away and only sporadic bursts of small guns cracked and jabbered. The men in the garage didn't know it then, but the fort had surrendered. The invisible chicks still cheeped between the silent groups. Occasionally a missioner would doze from sheer exhaustion and the day's horror, but he would come to with a start. Father Meyer grimly wriggled from his bonds and moved around the garage. Again he took charge and introduced a rhythm of order.

One by one, in spite of pain and numbness, the men dropped off. Hunger was forgotten in fitful sleep. In their exhaustion some of the men rolled over on the chicks until only one remained, somewhere in a far corner, plaintively piping, somewhat like a cricket. The men awoke before dawn, their throats parched. Some called for water. The guard came in with a canteen half full but would not turn it over until one of the men gave him in payment a gold wrist watch that the looters had overlooked at the house. The water allowed each man a brief sip, the guard holding the canteen to the men's lips. Hours later another canteen was handed in and each missioner had another swallow.

New groups of Japanese, passing the spot, came in to

look over the prisoners. Most of them just stood in the door and laughed in scorn; to them it was the proud white man a prisoner. Outside, now, there was no gunfire, only the occasional roar of fighters and bombers coming and going in the sky, the cries of Japanese working parties, the rumble of heavy trucks. At four o'clock in the afternoon a soldier brought in a tin of hard biscuit and a small can of condensed milk for each prisoner.

Late that afternoon the missioners heard English voices from another small building, next to the garage, where a score of British soldiers were under guard. Toward sundown a Japanese detail started digging grave-like pits while the missioners watched. Deep silence settled in their damp chamber again, and the English voices next door died away, too. All the men thought this could mean but one thing. The Japanese started crackling bonfires in the pits. The haggard captives' next thought was that they were to be consumed on these pyres, but Japanese soldiers lugged the bodies of their own dead to the pits and cremated them there. This was the last picture in the men's sight when they dropped off to sleep again that night, still bound.

Their wrists were raw at daybreak. The bonds had broken through the skin. Father Meyer talked long and earnestly with a Japanese officer who stopped in about that time and the officer ordered the guards to cut the bonds. The missioners chafed around their wrists, worked their arms and legs to get out stiffness and to revive circulation. The officer even permitted a brief period of calisthenics. The prisoners went through the exercises somewhat shakily, but the sense of motion warmed them and they were grateful for it. For breakfast that morning they finished their condensed milk and hard-tack. Later that morning the diet was enriched by a full bucket of water from a nearby well. The reservoir was still turned off.

Several missioners, at Father Meyer's behest, were permitted to go back to Stanley House under guard to fetch back several cans of tomato juice, coffee and biscuit. They got kohlrabi from the Maryknoll truck garden and a load of clothing. In the meantime, Father Meyer rigged a makeshift fireplace outside the garage and cooked the hard-tack and kohlrabi in tomato juice. An oil tin, scrubbed with sand, was the cooking pot. The condensed milk tins served for crockery. The hot meal worked wonders. Spirits lifted and the garage was policed. The heaps of potshards and odds and ends of metal and rubble were pushed to the walls. Grass stuffed into burlap bags made mattresses of a kind.

With the island completely in their hands, most of the Japanese gradually relaxed. Some came into the garage to try their imperfect English on the missioners. They were vainglorious and assured the missioners that Japan would rule not only the Pacific, but the whole world. Through Major Kerr, a British officer who had been pressed into service by the Japanese as interpreter, and a high-ranking Japanese officer, more missioners were sent back to Maryknoll House to bring down cases of canned foods. Major Kerr arranged to have the Maryknollers shifted from the cement garage floor to the wooden floor upstairs.

The missioners were sitting on the floor in their new quarters playing word games—"ghost," mostly—when word came that they were to be allowed to return to Maryknoll House. They got to their feet, formed at the door and

were marched up the hill to the lawn. Here they were kept
standing or sitting on the grass until dark. The weather was
mild, fires still burned around the island's rim and in the
center of Hong Kong, but the smoke sank steadily. Japanese
soldiers still occupied the house when the missioners were
admitted.

The lower floor was a shambles. The missioners aired
it, swept and scrubbed the tiles, threw out debris and other
accumulations. The Japanese kept the upper floors. The
missioners slept that night on the tiles downstairs between
their altars. There were no blankets and only a few re-
trieved the cassocks that had been torn from them when
they were first tied up, but they slept deeply because of
the quiet and freedom from bonds. The cooks managed to
dish up a fairly decent stew of various odds and ends and
that warmed them.

Next day, after the Japanese quit the upper floors, the
missioners rushed upstairs to see what they had left. The
sight was disheartening. Garments, papers, books, food
tins, bottles, religious articles were almost knee deep in
some places. Door panels had been splintered, beds were
missing, drawers had been pulled out and they and their
contents scattered. Father Meyer supervised another clean-
up. The men labored all day, and into the night, restoring
order as best they could. Their meals—they found several
bags of beans, some tinned stuff, sugar and rice—were
cooked on an improvised brick oven on the lawn. They
slept on the tiles again that night, but this time there were
some blankets to share.

Several days were passed in tireless labor before the
building took on some semblance of former neatness and

cleanliness. City water came on again and scrubbing proceeded apace. In a supply closet on an upper floor, when the door was pulled open, the priests found a wounded coolie. He had been in the closet four or five days without food or water. He died in Father Meyer's arms, a few days later. Linens and vestments were found intact and many chalices were recovered, but some had been battered and crushed by Japanese who had used them as ordinary drinking vessels. One by one the Chinese house-boys drifted back. They told hair-raising accounts of what had happened to them and to white civilians in Hong Kong.

Maryknoll House returned to routine, except that vigil lights and other candles and three oil lamps gave the only illumination at night. The Hong Kong power plant had been wrecked. The candle supply was low and the missioners had no idea how long it might be before the power would come on, or more candles be available. They retired early each night. Japanese guards patrolled the house and no man could leave without permission. Day by day, after New Year's, the food supply dropped lower and lower. On the morning of the thirteenth the last prunes were gone. The breakfast menu was reduced to coffee and hard-tack. Father William Downs kept a brief diary of these days:

Jan. 6:—Our sick men go to Queen Mary Hospital. Father Toomey accompanies them. Language classes again under way.

Jan. 13:—Now we have only oatmeal and coffee for breakfast. Hard-tack used up.

Jan. 14:—We received word we must go to an internment camp. We hurriedly gather together a few suitcases full of clothes and bundles of bedding. Await marching orders.

Jan. 16:—Still waiting word to leave. We have only part of a bag of rice left and only a few beans. Our servants, Ah Foung and Ah Tchin express willingness to share our fortunes, but we cannot keep them, or take them with us.

Jan. 19:—Still waiting for word.

Early in the afternoon, on January 20, the Maryknoll men plodded down the hill with their belongings. They were compelled, for lack of transportation, to leave behind many things that would have added comfort in internment. As they moved off, the older men looked back from the bottom of the hill at Maryknoll House perched on the crest and their hearts were heavy. Japanese guards herded them into Blocks E2, F and G in Stanley Prison.

2

STANLEY PRISON CAMP was an unlovely place. Approaching it from their hill, the missioners saw Japanese guards pacing outside the high barbed wire, their omnipresent bayonets glinting in the sun. Rubble and dust lay in unsightly heaps where bombs and shells had hit St. Stephen's College and the prison itself. Yawning shell and bomb craters were constant reminders of the devastation that had kept Hong Kong in terror for twenty days and nights. The missioners saw a string of Canadian soldiers, tied to one another with thick rope, plod across an open field under sullen little guards who kept shrilling, lunging at them with the ever-ready stickers. It made them a little ill. They knew

what it meant to live under constant threat of disembowel-
ment.

Inside the wire, the guards rudely assigned the missioners to their places. Four to seven were placed in each of
the bare chambers on the third floor in what had been the
prison warden's quarters. There were a few chairs, but
not nearly enough to go around, but there were camp cots
and, under the baleful glare of their captors the men set
these up and stowed their few possessions in corners of the
rooms. In the morning other internees lugged in a few
tables. These were to serve as altars. When the guards left
the building, British civilians came to greet the newcomers
and swapped yarns of their experiences. The missioners
noticed that all these men and women already showed signs
of grave physical deterioration from lack of proper food
and medical care. The children were hollow-cheeked and
hollow-eyed, suffering from malnutrition. They had seen
things never meant for childish eyes, much less adult vision.

The indefatigable Father Meyer, never one to daydream
or stand helpless in the face of what seemed an impossible
set-up, conducted a quick survey of the internment camp.
He marked a spot at St. Stephen's School where bombs had
torn away the corner of a brick building. He dug around
in the rubble heap and found bricks and parts of bricks
that might be used. "They'll make a good oven, if nothing
else," he decided. "We'll remember this brick pile." He
salvaged planking from bombed structures to make shelves,
more tables, benches and storage bins.

With Brother William T. Neary, a Pittsfield, Mass.,
Maryknoll man, he decided that a garage next door to the
warden's quarters would make an ideal communal kitchen.

Brother William, a wizard with tools, mortar and brick, fell to his task, and within a month had rigged an astonishingly adequate kitchen and dining hall in the garage. A group of stranded American merchant seamen and a host of British civilians stared goggle-eyed at Brother William's and Father Meyer's propensity for labor. One elderly British gentleman couldn't withhold admiring comment. "Bit of a Robinson Crusoe about that padre," he murmured. "Does miracles with the oddest bits."

It was all very well to have a neat kitchen and a sturdy dining table with benches, but with Hong Kong's disorganized million inhabitants to feed, the Japanese were not generous with rations to cook in the oven and set on the table. In the beginning there was barely enough for two meals a day, nor were these meals enough to put weight on a man. At ten o'clock in the morning there was weak coffee, served in tomato tins and a weak gruel of mixed rice and oatmeal. Father Meyer contrived, every few days, to have the cook make some kind of stew, but even this was watery. There was next to no meat the first few weeks of internment. He had carefully conserved some tins of bully beef. This gave the stews meat flavor, but the meat itself was virtually dissolved in order that it might be made to go around.

There were around 2,500 British men, women and children in cramped quarters throughout the camp, some 324 Americans, 50 Dutch men and women. There was talk, when the missioners started to circulate among their neighbors, of a prospective increase in rations, but this rumor, like the countless other rumors that developed, was a long time reaching fulfillment. During January and February

the bread ration was eight loaves to 324 Americans, or a
bite a day for each internee. The rice ration was eight
ounces, some days, but cooks were warned by Father
Meyer never to exhaust a full day's ration. The next day
rice might fail to come, or there would be less of it. On
such days the cook had to swell the rice with water and
serve it in a glutinous paste to have enough to go around.
Most nights the missioners fell into bed too weak to stand.
Canker sores broke out on their lips. Dysentery was common. This was general throughout the camp.

The men lost weight rapidly. Father Meyer brooded over
this until he figured out a way to supply vitamins to com-
bat the condition. He searched lawns and fields for alfalfa,
grass and such plants as he knew to be edible. These were
the only greens available and they were something less
than palatable, but he was grim in his insistence that the
men eat the stuff. It helped. Wild greens were better than
no greens at all. The Iowan even saved bones that came with
the rare rations of meat. When the bones were dried he
ground them with stones to get calcium and the Maryknoll
men drank the powder in water. He felt convinced that thus
he would save their teeth.

To the priests' astonishment, faithful Ah Tschin and Ah
Foung turned up at the camp one morning in early January. They presented themselves to Father Meyer with two
fish heads they had salvaged from the garbage heap outside
the hut where the American seamen lived. Father Meyer
was delighted. He scrubbed and washed the fish heads,
scraped every last fibre of flesh from them and with proper
seasoning, served a hot fish chowder that night that filled

the dining hall with aroma and had the starved missioners licking their chops.

The seasoning, incidentally, was another Robinson Crusoe creation. Frequently the daily ration lacked salt. Father Meyer had the men go to the beach each day to fill shallow tins with sea water. These tins were left on the roof in the hot sun and in due time the sun absorbed the water and left a salty residue. It was a slow but sure process. British, Dutch and other internees were inclined to scoff at first, but when they saw it worked, Stanley Prison rooftops blossomed out with pans of sea water.

Ah Tschin and Ah Foung swept, cleaned and helped collect branches, boards and twigs for fuel. They didn't mind sharing camp hardships and the meagre camp diet. The missioners had only a few dollars among them, but with this money Ah Tschin and Ah Foung went to Hong Kong to bargain for a few additional items for the Maryknoll larder. They were happy in this assignment, but the Japanese guards always grumbled on their return, sometimes kept them outside the high wire for hours in the hot sun. Each day the two Chinese boys found it more difficult to get in, once they had gone out. On the night of January 27th, they didn't show up again. The missioners returned to the diet of boiled mush, wild greens and watery stew.

Meanwhile the Maryknoll men had joined the general camp community. Internees of other faiths who had always assumed that all padres are hard, stern men of religion, were astonished to learn that they love to sing, play athletic games, and that they can entertain as well as be entertained. Father Arthur Allie of Two Rivers, Wisc., a Korean missioner in Hong Kong for hospital treatment, sat at the battered old upright on the community center, night after night, playing popular music for community songfests. Father Frank Keelan of Waverly, Mass., was chosen co-chairman of the camp's athletic committee and got up exciting soft ball games, hockey matches in which the sticks were tree limbs and the pucks were stones. Father Toomey was elected treasurer.

Some of the Japanese guards could not resist watching Father Keelan pitch. It turnéd out they had played on the diamond in Japan and were anxious to perfect certain curve balls. Father Keelan taught them and they seemed grateful. On the other hand, they earnestly assured him that baseball was of Japanese origin. "Americans learned from Japanese," they assured him. Father Keelan didn't argue the point.

Food was the main topic of conversation wherever internees assembled. The only food that came with unfailing regularity was the bread and milk for babies brought in each morning by a Red Cross truck. Frequently much of the stuff that was sent in for adults was tainted, or otherwise unfit for human consumption for some other reason, especially meats and fish. Stewards in other parts of the camp less ingenious than Father Meyer threw away soy beans that looked a little off color. He picked out these poorer beans, roasted them and served them as one would serve roasted peanuts. They were palatable in this form, and constituted a valuable food reserve.

On several occasions, starving civilians in Hong Kong hi-jacked loads of food bound for the camp. These civilians were starving themselves and in the face of starvation, conscience dissolved. On the morning of February 5th, even the Red Cross truck was stopped in the streets, and hi-jackers drove off the truck and its contents. Ration robberies were not infrequent in camp where stores were not adequately guarded. Because of this an American patrol was set up in camp and robberies were reduced. The main patrol post lay along a narrow dirt path back of the three American internment blocks. To make the camp sound a bit more like home this thoroughfare was called "Roosevelt Avenue."

Father Meyer tried to vary the menu when the men tired of looking at plain rice. He dug up a recipe for rice pancakes one morning and when these met with general favor, he managed to get them out two times a week. With the oatmeal and the meagre supply of flour—this was wormy and had to be sifted for weevils—he made a satisfactory dough that turned up on the tables in the form of buns. Fuel for cooking was a problem, but he stumbled across a heap of coal dust in the camp. This he converted into bricks, with mud and dry grass as filler, and the bricks, while slow to ignite, gave good heat.

Many of the inventions thought up by this amazing man were passed on to other groups in the internment camp who had seen the same materials without dreaming what possibilities they held. Father Meyer created a yeast from sweet potatoes, leaves, and a culture from the last cake of professional yeast left in the camp. Father Meyer's product was kept in milk bottles. Sometimes the pressure from the fermenting yeast blew the tops off the bottles and startled the missioners in their sleep. They never quite forgot the sound of rifle fire, and this sound was somewhat like it. Father

Meyer distributed the yeast and a bread recipe to house-wives in the camp.

To conserve fuel, this priestly da Vinci created a man-sized thermos jug of a large coolie basket, and a crock wrapped in rags and sheathing that kept liquids, meats and vegetables hot for hours after they left the stove. When the Japanese, after several months, permitted internees to bathe in the sea, Father Meyer solved the bathing suit problem by cutting a pattern for trunks that could be made from old toweling. He taught the idle to carve chessmen and checkers, made toys for the children, and within a few months had truck gardens going. Even the most stolid British in the camp looked on him with a degree of awe. "That incredible man," they called him. It was the ulti-mate in compliments. Nothing less described him.

In spite of all his care and ingenuity, however, sickness overtook the Maryknoll men as it did others. None of the missioners lost less than five pounds a month. At the end of six months, the Iowa padre had lost fifty of his two hundred pounds. Priests and brothers along with men, women and children from other parts of the camp were in and out of the hospital that had been set up for them. Father Tackney, weak and suffering from low blood pres-sure, took to fainting dead away. Deaths were numerous in the camp, especially among children and older prisoners. There was only one coffin in the camp. This was used for all funerals. Burials were in burlap sacks. Stanley boun-dary stones were converted into headstones. Brief, crude epitaphs were carved into them.

A Maryknoll diary of these grim events tells the story: *March 5:*—A Mr. Walsh of the Hong Kong police dies. . . . Buried after open-air requiem on tennis court. Body escorted to old military cemetery on The Hill. Some graves date from 1845.

March 8:—Father Toomey preaches. Afternoon service as usual. Special menu because this is Sunday. Three rice pancakes, minute pieces of bacon. Supper, hash, beans, rice, no bread.

March 16:—Father Vincent Walsh suddenly ill. Father Haughey gets face slapped. Failed to be in vicinity of block at 7 P.M. as Japanese regulations require.

March 18:—No soy beans rationed since Feb. 24. Milk for babies and children reduced.

March 20:—Five escapes from camp during night, three Americans, two British. (Later number increased to eleven.) Spelling bee scheduled for this evening called off. Three thousand eggs arrived in camp. That means one apiece—if. Only one slice of bread every other day now, or less.

March 31:—Many now have only cup of hot water for breakfast. Seen around camp: Food in British kitchens served from wash basin, soup from former garbage cans. Bread carried from block to block on hospital stretchers. Burlap bags appear in place of shoes. Beards in profusion for lack of shaving utensils, toilet articles.

April 5:—Easter Sunday—Solemn Mass—9:30, congregation standing on lawn. Rumor has it we are all to be repatriated????

April 13:—Everybody hungry. Little camp activity. Soft ball, other games fallen off due to weakness. Even children listless. Doctors report 90 per cent of camp children suffering from malnutrition. Our piece of bread dwindles in size; three inches long, one inch wide.

Hollow-cheeked men and women tried to forget hunger in chess and bridge. Every bit of gossip from outside was eagerly discussed. Extravagant rumors provided food for hours of conversation. Hitler died a hundred times, in false accounts. Tokyo was wiped out repeatedly. Each time hope flared, only to die away again, then the more melancholy fell to deeper pits of depression. New rumors were discounted, eventually as "more bamboo wireless," and there were only a few things to hope for—an occasional basket of food from outside, an unexpected jump in the ration. Heavy, typhonic rains brought added despondency.

Occasionally the international canteen had American cigarettes for sale, but few of the missioners could buy these. They sold at $1 Hong Kong, and there was no money left to speak of. The men took to making cigarettes of old pine needles, used tea leaves, even from dried banyan and papaya leaves.

April 22:—Mr. Albert Simmons, former Stanley resident, died today. Heart failure brought on by malnutrition. Burial 6 P.M. in our cemetery which, by the way, has fair number of new graves. According to bamboo wireless we're going back to the States about June 1.

May 3:—Coffee and bun from Father Meyer's kitchen for breakfast. Father Meyer promises us bread three times a day—that is at least a bun—out of his five ounce flour allotment.

May 20:—Report *Asama Maru* may arrive here June 15, leave June 16, with repatriates. Meeting of Americans to discuss repatriation. Father Meyer decides he'll stay.

May 31:—Tiger seen in camp. One has been killed by police. Weighed 240 pounds, was three feet high. Mr. Fisher died in camp hospital.

June 23:—Our rice ration today very meagre. Father Meyer came to our rescue and we fared not too badly. He has been drying out and toasting left-over rice, keeping it for just such days as this. Rain.

June 29:—*Asama Maru* arrives off Stanley 12:30 P.M. Anchors mile off shore. Father Meyer prepares a tasty supper. His kitchen helpers are Fathers Keelan, Downs, Madison. Camp very quiet.

Quiet indeed, since there were but a few of the camp population, and these Americans, to board the *Asama*. A half dozen or so of the Maryknollers who were among the sickly left for Lorenzo Marques, East Africa, and then via the *S.S. Gripsholm* for home.

July 15:—Maryknoll Sister Henrietta Marie celebrates her feast day by giving us a piece of chocolate cake. Other food as usual. Water spinach wormy, tough. Chives— enough said. Heavy rains continue.

July 30:—A Miss Ross died today.

By now suits, as well as shoes, of burlap appeared in the camp. Now there was swimming off the prison beach and the interned men and women were grateful for the chance to cool off and keep clean. Bathing facilities had been meagre. It was September 12 before the Maryknoll men, mere shadows of the group that had laughed and eaten so heartily the night of December 7—how remote that day seemed—clambered weakly aboard the bus that was to take them into Hong Kong. Bishop Valtorta of Hong Kong received permission for them to reside with the French

Fathers near Hong Kong City. Eighteen in number, they took the road shortly after for mission duty in unoccupied China.

Only two Maryknoll men remained in the Stanley Prison Camp, Father Donald Hessler of Lake Orion in Michigan and Father Meyer. Before they left, the repatriated missioners wrung the hands of these two. Both had decided to remain to take care of the men, women and children still behind barbed wire though they could have moved out with the rest. Father Meyer discouraged emotionalism, but some of the men had to fight back tears and control the pressure at their throats.

The bus gears meshed. The freed ones moved slowly up hill and Father Meyer and Father Hessler, behind the wire and the sullen guards with the flashing bayonets, waved after them. On the bus, tears finally brimmed over. Constricted throats loosened in prayer for the men who had chosen to stay behind. Just before the bus turned a bend on the hill the missioners had their last look of the stocky superman from Iowa. He was striding purposefully across the grass in the attitude of a man who had things to do.

V

Jungle Padres

FATHER RAYMOND BONNER'S new jungle parish in Northeastern Bolivia lies next door to South America's notorious "Green Hell," wherefore, to hear some of his naive Indian parishioners tell it, the Devil spends more time creating mischief among them, his nearest neighbors, than he does elsewhere. The point came up recently one blazing afternoon when the padre stood on the Tauhuamanu River bank in torrid Filadelphia baptizing twenty-three Indian babies. His assistant at this ceremony was venerable Don Pedro who has been lay spiritual guide to the district for more than forty years, because there were no priests to penetrate this corner of the jungle. Infants at the font squirmed, whimpered, and contorted their faces in agonized screams, and sensationally-colored parrots, macaws and toucans swelled the racket with even more raucous obligato. Don Pedro gently plucked the perspiring young missioner's tropical white cassock. "Father," he murmured earnestly, "it is not really the children who cry; it is the little devil in each of them, protesting God's victory."

This quaint Indianism is mild compared with some the missioners encounter as, by dugout, canoe, motor launch, on donkeys and afoot, they make the rounds of Indian settlements hidden and all but buried in steaming jungle vegetation. Some Indian villages in the Bolivian Pando have not seen a priest in generations, some know of them only as a legend dating back to the Sixteenth Century Jesuits who accompanied the conquistadors among the Incas from whom many of these tribes are descended. Witch doctors and other primitive sorcerers oppose the Maryknoll men in the more remote settlements, and the missioners face death in some of their routine journeys, from outlaw tribesmen who are uncannily handy with blowgun and poisoned dart.

The American padres, who first came to South America from Maryknoll in 1942, in the Pando's litany of possible woes find bugs, sweat and fever, tremendous boa constrictors that are apt to slither to fatal embrace from overhanging boughs in jungle corridors. They face tigers, pumas, jaguars and wildcats on their routine treks. Alligators drool in the muddy rivers that are the missioners' highways, and enormous electric eels make it dangerous to suffer a spill in these turgid waters. On the trail the missioners live off game and fish, cooked over jungle campfires, and when such food is not available turn often to *charque*, a dried beef that isn't good even after they resignedly forgive its high odor. They are machine-age pioneers in a region where the Indian's life pattern has visibly changed but little in almost 1000 years.

The danger from great reptiles and wild animals is real. Father Bonner can attest to that. He is tall, dark-haired, the laughing type. He has made friends easily in the Pando, as he did at home. He was born in Philadelphia, Pa., a fact always borne in on him when he visits the Filadelphia in his own jungle parish. He caddied at Paxon Hollow Golf Course at Ardmore, Pa., in his boyhood. Anyway, he set out, one day, from the center in Cobija, to ride the jungle trail to Porvenir and Filadelphia, with only a lively *chico* to accompany him. They rode donkeys.

He found the jungle a bedlam as his donkey, head adroop, jogged along at rhythmic, philosophic gait. Monkeys squeaked and chattered in the lush and twisted vegetation that soars in live jade walls from the narrow trail. Macaws and parrots scolded harshly. Swarms of humming birds and an astonishing variety of other tiny feathered creatures flashed past like winged rubies, sapphires and emeralds. All about the young padre the jungle was boundless green gloom, except where the sun found openings and lanced through, blinding white.

Four hours out, the donkey shied at a hanging branch thicker than a man's arm—at least Father Bonner thought it was a branch until it coiled purposefully. The priest lifted his shotgun and the jungle corridors roared and reverberated to the explosion. A twelve foot boa thrashed frenziedly in death throes, and showered the trail with dank green leaves. The frightened *chico* was speechless. Finally, though, the boa lay still in the jungle humus and they moved on again.

The American youngsters who roam the steaming bottom lands in the Pando, knew before they left comfortable homes in all parts of the United States that they were to be—among other things—priests, doctors, nurses, pioneers, teachers, planters, overseers, storekeepers and veterinarians. They were aware of the dangers they would have to face. They knew, for example, that some of the Bolivian and other South American tribes still take a fancy to a white man's head. As recently as 1938, a band of wild Inaparis killed Father Arnaldo, O.P., who went to work among them. Part of his corpse was found later in the Madre de Dios River.

Father James Logue, a Maryknoll man in the Pando, heard from native parishioners the story about a Government telegrapher who was murdered by one of the lowland tribes. "Actually, padre," the narrators told him, innocently, "they meant him no harm. They only wanted the gold from his teeth for certain ornaments." Another time a withered tribesman displayed a flute made from a human forearm. The primitive musician obliged with a few melancholy notes and then went into the fine points of jungle flute manufacture. "Any forearm will do, of course," the wrinkled gaffer confided, "but it is established that a flute from a white man's arm gives a sweeter tone." These macabre practices, fortunately, are not universal.

Some idea of the quaint, primordial medicine that was practiced in these parts before the padres came with their portable dispensaries, is gleaned from a story told by Father Fred Walker of East Boston, Mass., who has the mission at Villa Victoria, not far from La Paz. He saw a pint-sized little girl in miserable dress lugging a large but mouldy cow's heart along the dusty road. It was clutched to her thin chest. She was barefoot and grimy, but her eyes were lively and bright. The padre was curious as to what she meant to do with the heart. "It is to keep at home," the child told him. "Old cow's heart is good for pneumonia."

Father Walker wondered whether the patient would have it cooked, or eat it raw. The child seemed ashamed for the padre's ignorance. "You do not eat it at all," she told him. "You press it against the affected lung and soon the lung is well again."

The men of Maryknoll have set up missions in Bolivia in the Chilean hills, the Peruvian highlands, among Central American Indians and along some parts of the seacoast of Ecuador. Many are one to two months' journey from the nearest railroad, and had to reach their stations by primitive water craft, astride donkeys and on foot through interminable forests. Many may be in the wilderness for at least a decade, far removed from other white men; others may never leave, preferring to keep their period of service unbroken. Some must swelter in lowlands heat, some live in Arctic temperature on Andean heights.

Soon after the new men took over their stations in the Pando, Father Thomas J. Danehy of Manitowoc, Wisc., submitted a report on the peoples' needs: "We expect to repay the kindness with which we have been received in this country," he set down, "by making up not only for the things that are lacking in the spiritual diet of the people, but also for the things lacking in the material diet. We have found a nervous, under-nourished people which should be the last thing in this lush land. We have seen prevalent here, malaria, typhoid, leprosy. Apart from these serious ailments, is the under-nourishment, which can be remedied. Although vegetables can be grown in abundance, few natives take advantage of the vitamin content of ordinary vegetables such as cabbage, carrots, lettuce, tomatoes, etc. Despite the number of cows that graze throughout the town

—even in the churchyard, when they can gain entrance—few children get anything like the proper amount of milk. Young and old alike have exceedingly poor teeth. It is only occasionally that we see a set of teeth that resemble God's gift to man." As fast as the new American missioners took over, they began work on these problems and have made promising headway.

Already, some of these, and other unhealthy conditions, are in a way to be remedied. Father John J. Lawler of New Bedford, Mass., startled natives near Riberalta when he submitted, soon after his arrival, to a blood transfusion to save a *niña*, a little native girl who lay dying. According to native superstition such rashness could have only one result—the donor must, of necessity, die with the patient. When the *niña* got back on her feet and Father Lawler kept hustling around as usual, local superstition went by the board. To the local doctor's delight, Indians swarmed in for blood typing and offered their names as blood donors.

Whooping cough, last spring, carried off 200 children, from thirty to forty a day in Riberalta, as it has done at intervals for generations. Indian children, because of unbalanced diet, succumb weakly to this ailment. Father Lawler, looked upon as a miracle-working padre, pleaded from the pulpit for parishioners to bring their children to Dr. Payne of the American Medical Commission, to receive injection against whooping cough. When it worked, Indians flooded out of the jungle to have their *niños* and *chicos* innoculated. These were things they had never heard of. The missioners treat tropical ulcers, pull teeth, encourage home sanitation. A group of Maryknoll Sisters are setting up a hospital in Cobija, the mission center.

Father Ambrose Graham, who works among the Indians in Cavinas, a remote river settlement, even turned in a good job as veterinarian not long ago. "The fellow who is taking this letter," he related in a recent missive to headquarters, "came running in on me tonight, shouting for help. His mule had been bitten by a viper. Think of the effect on my clientele if this mule should turn up his toes right at my door. I got out a bottle of kerosene for a purge, poured it down the mule's throat and cut around the spot where the viper had struck. The mule limps but is okay."

The Indians call on the new padres for everything, and the missioners seldom fail them. The natives, though, are apt to be a bit on the lazy side, due largely to the tropical climate. Few make enough to keep them alive. They wear dyed burlap skirts, cotton trousers held together by perpetual patching and only a minority are familiar with shoes. They carry on a primitive barter system. Father Graham—he's a New York City man—prodded his parishioners into tapping the wild rubber trees in which the region abounds and has arranged to get the stuff to market. It will eventually go into Allied Nations' war supplies. The jungle is rich in mahogany, rosewood, and other precious lumber which the natives had ignored because they had no lumbering tools. Their own homes are primitive bamboo shacks. Father Graham got saws and the lumber is stacking up at Cavinas.

"Indians here coming along nicely," Father Graham reported in another recent letter from Cavinas. "This group doesn't have too nice a history—tried to kill a padre with ground glass just a few years ago and a few years earlier another unfortunate priest walked into an arrow. Heard a few stories about one of the boys planning to do a job on me when he came in for the holidays. I sent for him and publicly asked him all about it. He denied the story, but the effect was swell. Everything going nicely since we showed up the local witch doctor by curing a man he'd almost killed. This is the second case we cleared up after the witch doctor had left a patient for dead. . . . Helped dull the Indian's fear of boa constrictors when I hunted a big baby in one of my rubber centrals yesterday. The snake wasn't there. The Indians said he was afraid of the padre and scrammed. Now they've gone back to work in that section. With a little encouraging I think many of these people will come to do better by themselves."

Father Graham and his partner, Father Gordon N. Fritz of Newport, Minn., have a temperamental one-lung power generator at their mission. When it works it feeds their electric light and radio. The Cavinas bring other Indians, from camps deeper in the jungle, to goggle in superstitious awe at the music, which they love, and at the witticisms of Jack Benny, Fred Allen and Fibber McGee, which they don't, of course, understand at all.

Some idea of the opportunities in these dark jungle parishes is conveyed in a summary of activities at Cavinas by Father Graham written in May, 1943, less than a year after he took over.

"I have been here, alone, with the Indians for some time. I have fifty families to take care of spiritually and temporally. I had to start virtually from scratch to build up industries. We are working on rubber, sugar cane, coffee, agriculture in general, a small tannery, a brick and tile plant and we have some cattle. I must persuade the men to build more than seventy houses, plus a church and a rectory. The launch that connects us with civilization drops in to disturb our peace on the average of once every two months, at times the period is stretched to three months. What we need here is an airport and we may get around to it. Then I have, virtually, to buy freedom for more than twenty families that live in heavy debt working rubber for the whites outside. I am having a lot of fun here in the wilderness."

Curious native customs intrigue the young missioners. Father Lawler's first native burial among the Calacala Indians, for example, was rather weird. It was the funeral of a man who had reached the astonishing age of ninety-five years. Around the nailed coffin clustered the women of the family, dressed in black, except for the white derby which is part of the Indians' everyday dress. The padre's ritual for the dead had hardly begun before the women cut in with piercing screams. "It was not the shrieking cry of the professional mourner," Father Lawler says, "nor yet the emotional sobbing of grief." He was astonished to learn that this wailing is sternly forbidden to any but immediate members of the family. For even a beloved friend to horn in is considered extremely bad taste.

A little boy marched ahead of the coffin on the way to the burial ground at Queru-Queru, an hour's walk from the house, over narrow mud tracks and across fields of grass face-high. Whenever the pall-bearers stopped for a breather, the little boy slipped the table under the coffin and members of the family threw themselves on the box and got on with their peculiar wailing, or keening. Just before the coffin was lowered into the grave, the family tore off the lid and kissed the old father farewell. None but the family folk had this privilege, either. The burial was followed by a sort of wake at which family and other mourners did pretty well for themselves with a couple of casks of *Chicha*, the native drink. The pattern wailing, incidentally, broke off abruptly after the coffin was lowered.

Another morning, Father Lawler came to bless a new Indian home. The only furniture was a crude bed, a table and the single chair which was set aside strictly for the padre's use. It was not long after dawn, and breakfast had not been served, but murderous cocktails of native distillation were passed around and Father Lawler had to take one. The idea of a snorting cocktail before breakfast made the missioner unhappy but he brightened when he caught on that it is native custom to dash part of the drink to the earthen floor, before sipping. He got rid of most of his that way, and felt a little better. His relief was brief, though. There was a second—different, but no less potent —cocktail, and a glass of native beer to put down before he could get on with the blessing. Most of this went to the floor, like the first. "Noble custom, dashing some of the stuff on the ground," Father Lawler decided.

At Baturite, on the Bolivian side of the Rio Acre, Father Gerard Grondin, a Westbrook, Me., man, witnessed a fantastic all-night jungle wedding. The Indians lighted tremendous bonfires in their clearing and set two pigs and a great bull on the barbecue pits. A blind Indian guitarist who roams the water-ways, performs at fiestas and weddings and gives one-man concerts at lonely *barracas*, was the only musician. He played primeval Indian melodies and dance tunes, and the unshod guests gracefully tripped it on the spongy jungle floor. *Niños* and *chicos* shrieked and darted between the dancers, having a great time, as all small fry do at weddings, and the firelight created ominous blocks of great shadows on the frowning green, jungle walls. There was native liquor, but the wedding party never degenerated into an orgy. The party lasted through sun-up.

In Calacala, the Sunday before Lent, Maryknoll padres ran into a quaint and rather damp local version of the North American Hallowe'en. Instead of flour, though, the *niños, chicos* and their elders used water. For weeks before the carnival the children saved up egg-shells, which they loaded with water, plugging the holes with dough. When the eggs ran out, they used home-made balloons filled with water. In the final phases of the fiesta, they just dumped the water on passersby from pitchers or buckets. This ceremony is the *"mojada,"* or, *"the drenching."* The community small fry formed self-appointed guard groups to run ahead of the padres, calling out, "He who forgets himself, he will have cause to regret." The drenching ended just before dinner, leaving time for change of garments. The poorer folk, who own only one shabby outfit, entered the little church dripping.

Among the Quechas in Calacala, rule is matriarchal. On St. John's day the inhabitants, led by withered women elders, paraded the dusty streets with a life-size painting of the saint. Flanking marchers walked with lighted candles, and with smoking incense. In the little church the head-woman offered up small ceremonial loaves of St. John's bread, made especially for this day, in token of that saint's aid to the sick and the poor. After the loaves were blessed, they were eaten, the idea behind it presumably being, that those who had partaken of the loaves would be kept from hunger by St. John during the following year. Outside the church, fireworks were exploded on signal from the ancient head-woman who squatted in the place of honor, on the floor in front of all the others.

All in all, Calacala parish keeps fairly lively. On St. Patrick's day, of all days, shrill children stirred Father Lawler from his midday meal to fight a huge serpent that had wormed its way down the church aisle to the sacristy. Father Lawler caught up a cudgel, went into the church, and cautiously looked for the intruder. Barefoot children tip-toeing after him on the first floor, all prepared to turn and run should the snake head for them. It turned out, though, that between the time they ran for the padre and got back again, the snake had slithered out and vanished. Nevertheless the tale of the priest's bold hunt got around as all local gossip does, with incredible swiftness. It was neighborhood talk for days.

When the new priests first came, they found it difficult to get accustomed to the distractions that make the average Indian devotions something less than peaceful. Indian mothers always bring their young strapped to their backs and before a Mass is ended, the missioners have to compete with the strident wails of these jungle offspring. The grave elders have an informal way of moving right up as he preaches. *Niños* get a bit shrill and quarrelsome, sometimes, and even the village mongrels, of which there are astonishing numbers, occasionally chase one another around between their worshipping owners. "It's a little upsetting in the beginning," some of the missioners admit, "but you get used to it."

In Villa Victoria, Father Flaherty's Aymara parishioners are, if anything, even poorer than the tribes in other parishes. So far, there is no church. Service is held under the sky. The padre walks abroad before each Mass, ringing the hand bell as a call to devotions, and tattered children swarm about him on the rounds. Some of the children act as self-appointed interpreters and echo Father Flaherty's words as he stops in at the little mud houses with a personal invitation to each family to come to prayer. Some of the children run ahead, eagerly giving notice that, "the padresito comes, the padresito comes." "My apostles," Father Flaherty calls them.

Poverty is so extreme in this parish that the Indians seldom have anything for the collection plate. They are eager for a church of their own, though, and in lieu of funds they lug to Sunday Mass such adobe bricks as they have time to make during the week. These are left at the spot where the church is eventually to stand. Meanwhile, at service the Indians use the unset mud bricks instead of pews, and worship with full heart. They assure the pastor that when there is enough brick, they will work on red tile for the roof. One ancient walked from the service with the padre one morning in philosophical mood. "Bricks, padresito, can be made with water and with clay," he told Father James Flaherty, "but bolivianos (Bolivian currency) cannot, sometimes be made even with sweat and with tears."

In another community, some distance beyond Villa Victoria, Father Walker was astonished to find a priestless congregation that had built its own chapel and maintained it for years against the day when a padre might come. The interior was decorated with thirty extraordinarily beautiful native paintings and was immaculate, in contrast with some of the houses of worship in this territory. On the evening before Mass the village mayor, a sturdy Indian with dark stiff hair that looked more or less like a startled mop, climbed the hill of the village and in loud, clear baritone, chanted the Indian church call. He repeated this on the hour. Father Walker could not remember that he had ever heard a more beautiful voice. He heard it again at Mass as the tousle-haired mayor led the congregation in the chanting of lovely, simple Aymara hymns.

Bishop Alonso M. Escalante of the Maryknoll Pando Mission is a vivacious, bespectacled little man, born in Merida in Mexico, who has been a Maryknoller the past twenty-three years. He is a naturalized American citizen. Like all the missioners with him in Bolivia, he maintains humble quarters, hardly more modern than those in which his parishioners dwell. Choice of a man of Latin American birth who knows Spanish and takes easily to the bewildering dialects of the jungle folk pleased official Bolivia. Bishop Escalante understands these people, since they resemble his own. He was consecrated, incidentally, at the Shrine of Our Lady of Guadalupe in Mexico.

Bishop Escalante has more than a decade of mission work already behind him. He worked a long time in Manchuria. A practical enthusiast, he has tremendous plans for the Pando. When conditions permit, he intends to put motor launches into service on the great rivers and back waters that connect his Pando stations. Such a service will keep the men supplied with agricultural implements, seed and building materials so that the Indians may have the wherewithal to lift themselves, with the padres' aid, from the deep poverty in which they have wallowed hopelessly so many years.

Bishop Escalante entered his new field with character-istic humility, not with the brashness of that species of tourist or commercial promoter from which jungle natives as well as cultured officials are so apt to shrink. He has set his course in the Pando along the lines suggested by Bishop James E. Walsh, Maryknoll's Superior General, made after Bishop Walsh had personally surveyed the field. The nub of this suggestion was:

"Always remember, we are not going as exponents of so-called North American civilization. As regards the ele-ments of true civilization, we expect to receive as much as we give." This sensible approach, humbly set forth by the society's head, struck just the right note. Bolivian official-dom as well as the local clergy, heard it with obvious de-light.

The humble attitude is not confined to words. When a poor Indian family was burned out of its home one night in Cobija, Father Bonner took in the whole family—father, mother and children. The rectory in Cobija has only three rooms, but Father Bonner saw to it that his guests had com-fort. His generosity had instant effect on the populace. Relatives of the homeless Indians and Cobijan officials, perhaps a little ashamed that they had not taken in the destitute group, got together and immediately started work on a new home for the family.

It is a lonely life, but the missioners are geared for it.

Though months go by, sometimes, before they see another white man, they occasionally meet parties of American rubber hunters or men sent out by such groups as the Rockefeller Foundation. These are red-letter days, something to write home about. Father Bonner was walking in Cobija one afternoon when he ran into—of all people—Orson Welles. They shook hands and talked of home. The visitor explained that he had come down with a Rockefeller commission which plans to spend a large sum for health improvement in South America. The impresario confided that he had no official duty in this connection. "Just bummed the ride," he told Father Bonner.

In Villa Victoria, last April, the mission went into a dither when word came through that a great Americano might drop in for a visit. Father Flaherty and Father Walker got children and adults to fill ditches and wagon ruts. The streets were swept in a fury of rising dust. Finally, the guest rode down the street with Bolivian officials, and the women of Villa Victoria set up a barrage of rich jungle blossoms. The inspection party stayed only a little while, but just before it left the great Americano threw one arm around Father Walker's shoulder. "It's great to see the old American spirit down this way," he said. Pretty soon, the guests were gone again. The Aymaras crowded excitedly around Father Walker, wonder distending their dark eyes. "The great Americano is your friend, padre?" they wanted to know. Father Walker grinned. He had never met the great Americano before. It was Vice President Henry Wallace.

VI

Death on a Mountain

GERARD, SON OF MICHAEL DONOVAN, mechanic, was born in McKeesport, a Pittsburgh suburb on the Monongahela, on October 14, 1904. He was the youngest of seven sons and daughters, a puny flaxen-haired kid, distinguished by an unchanging mischievous grin. His hair kept falling into his eyes and his prattle was constant. He looked pretty much as Mickey Rooney looked, when Mickey Rooney was a boy in the films.

The McKeesport Donovans lived modestly at the foot of Converse Street on the cliffs that overlook the Youghiogheny Valley. When the boy wasn't reading, he looked from his window through flame-blacked smoke from the steel and iron mills that writhed and hovered over tireless hearths and crucibles. The smoke cast spells over him. He weaved dreams out of it.

The Donovans were devout. One sister, Nonnie, was a nun. Joe was already destined for the priesthood. It followed, more or less, that the youngest child might enter the church, too, and eventually he did. He went to Maryknoll Seminary after Joe had been ordained there. Tom, a third member of the family, eventually became a Maryknoller after Joe. Mary Donovan, their mother, was quietly proud of her sons.

Father Gerard Donovan left the United States for Fushun in Manchukuo, his first mission assignment, in the Spring of 1931. He was twenty-seven years old.

Early letters from Manchukuo, near the Siberian-Korean border, were only slightly nostalgic. The young missioner saw romance in the vast forests and in the towering mountains there. The Manchus, Chinese, and Koreans fascinated him. His letters showed obvious worship of older missioners and of their achievements and adventures in this weird, new land.

"I wish," he wrote to his sister Kate in the Fall of 1931, a few months after he got to Fushun, "that you could see the Winter outfit I am getting, a blanket-lined cassock, padded trousers, woolen socks, woolen underclothes, fur overcoat, fur gloves and fur hat and skate shoes to accommodate several pairs of woolen socks. It seems ridiculous to get these things now when the sun is warm, but soon there will be a different story."

Letters kept coming to McKeesport on faithful schedule. Kate read them to Michael Donovan and to her mother, sometimes to the neighbors. They described Chinese foods —*chao tze,* a kind of meatball done in flour batter and soya sauce, *pai tsai,* a cabbage dish, and the tiny cups of tea served at all Chinese meals. One letter described the *k'ang,* a kind of mud-brick stove that served not only for cooking, but for bed and table, too, when weather was severe.

In late Fall, in 1931, young Donovan rode out to the

mission at Hsin Pin with Father Frank Bridge. From the back of a sturdy Mongolian pony, as they jogged along, he marvelled at the wild beauty of the country. "Our road wound up and over mountains the like of which you have never seen outside of movies, then mile after mile through pleasant valleys, crossing and recrossing the same winding river. In places we had to keep our feet up to save a wetting."

Father Donovan did not share the common uneasiness about roving bandits who swept down on village and town, sometimes in little groups, sometimes in small armies, to loot and kill. Kate and his parents though, kept asking about them in their letters. His answers were always reassuring. "Over here," he told them, "we don't worry about them as you do at home. They haven't bothered any of our men because we're Americans."

His confidence was somewhat misplaced, as it turned out. One afternoon late in the Summer of 1932, two robber groups exchanged fire in Hsin Pin. Bullets shattered the mission windows, sent roof tiles clattering, thudded against the mud walls. No one in the mission was hurt, but for almost an hour while the air echoed to shrill Chinese battle-cries and gunfire explosion, the mission staff including terror-stricken native assistants, hugged the floors with passionate embrace. Father Donovan didn't mention this in his letters to McKeesport.

Not long afterward Father Bridge came low with an illness that left him almost blind. Doctor Leggate, the kindly Scottish physician from the nearby Presbyterian mission, finally talked Father Bridge into leaving for what they called "outside." He helped natives lift Father Bridge into one of the two-wheeled springless carts that are common to the region, and they started the two-day trek to the railroad. Father Donovan, fighting the lumps in his throat, but outwardly smiling, walked a few miles with the cart.

Finally, he leaned over the recumbent pain-racked figure. He said, "Good-bye, Frank. I'll be waiting for you." Father Bridge smiled back. "So long, Jerry," he said. "I'll be seeing you." The wheels creaked and the cart moved slowly on. Father Donovan watched until it had plunged out of sight over a low ridge. He walked slowly back to the mission and the tears that slid down the boyish face were not started by the moaning wind, nor the biting snow. Frank Bridge and Jerry Donovan were not to meet again this side of heaven.

There's more to work in the field, Father Donovan soon learned, than the routine. A few weeks after Father Bridge had vanished over the ridge, a Catholic mother and daughter came to the mission with a difficult problem. When the girl was a baby she had been promised to a boy in her village whose family had paid ninety dollars for her as betrothal guarantee. Later the boy had left the village to become the Manchurian equivalent of a hobo.

"We thought, *Shen Fu*, that he had left the village forever," the mother explained. "Tender Blossom has taken another. Now the first one, after eight years, has returned. Tender Blossom does not want him, but we lack the full amount the village elders have awarded him as judgment."

Tender Blossom's new love was a Christian; the man who had bought her in childhood, was not. Father Donovan settled the case in his own way. "I know what a feeble-brained wretch you'll believe me," he wrote to Monsignor Lane, head of the district, "but I saw no other way out." Monsignor Lane understood. The fifty-six dollars that Father Donovan had paid out of the Hsin Pin Mission funds was refunded from the Fushun treasury. At the wedding in his chapel Father Donovan was rewarded by Tender Blossom's ecstatic smile.

The tattered Robin Hoods around Hsin Pin grew more active each passing day. In spite of Father Donovan's confidence that they wouldn't be apt to harm Americans, they wounded the Rev. Mr. Henderson, a Methodist minister in the settlement. The Hsin Pin elders dug a great moat around the village and built mud ramparts to stave off further attacks, but to no purpose. The robbers, mostly inferior marksmen, startled the Maryknoll Mission one afternoon when a wild shot hit, and rang, the chapel bell.

About one year after Father Bridge had gone, Father Donovan set out on the mission circuit in his place. He rode alone or with a terrified Chinese assistant, to isolated hamlets on the forest's edge and in the mountains, often to Huai-Jen, sixty miles from Hsin Pin, through country swarming with Manchu trigger men. He loved this life. His letters to McKeesport described it almost rapturously. There was still a lot of boy in the missioner.

In December, 1934, he rode back to Hsin Pin through snow waist high from another visit to Huai-Jen, and presided at the Christmas service. "Our little chapel was a gem by candlelight," he wrote glowingly to Kate, "though it looked crude by day. The straw-thatched crib, snowy linen on the altar, red-cassocked, slanty-eyed altar boys— all these made the perfect setting for the Midnight Mass of my boyhood dreams. I would not trade it for the most gorgeous cathedral in Christendom."

The following March—Waking-of-Insects-Month they call it in Manchukuo—Monsignor Lane detailed Jerry Donovan to Lin Kiang, the society's most remote outpost. It was a journey of more than six hundred miles by railroad and mule, yet actually less than 200 miles, straight-line, from Hsin Pin. Wang Yun Chang, a native assistant, rode along on the trek. The boy from McKeesport was delighted with the new post. Lin Kiang, a great lumber center, had crude electric lighting but twenty minutes outside the town, as Father Donovan put it in a letter home, "you are back 2,000 years."

Chinese from south of the Great Wall had tried to settle the district, but many had been frightened off by robber bands and had trekked back again. This was a country for lumber-jacks not for tillers of the soil.

The little padre and his native helper rode up one great mountain, down another on trips around the wilderness circuit. They stopped at little villages that had never seen a priest, nor any other white man. But Chinese immigrants in these little settlements recognized the cassock. They found one family in the wilderness that maintained a little chapel in their three-room house. Father Donovan was inspired by such examples of faith. He ignored all physical obstacles to penetrate deeper and deeper into the wilds.

Sung Shu Chen, a valley hamlet in the Lin Kiang circuit was a problem community. Manchu and Chinese dwellers there neglected their stock and their crops to dream the hours away with poppy poison. It wasn't simply this, though, that worried Father Donovan's helper. "The elders in Sung Shu Chen," Wang told the priest one day, "have commanded that all the village folk, including our parishioners, devote a certain number of days' labor to building a temple to Confucius. Our parishioners have refused."

The little man from McKeesport rode into Sung Shu Chen, exchanged politenesses with the local mandarin and gradually worked around to asking whether the temple was intended as a house of religious worship—idol worship, he meant, though he didn't call it that. The mandarin knew what the smiling padre was getting at. The edifice, he explained, was to be a shrine to a great scholar to encourage the village folk to study.

"The Kingly way of Confucius, Father," he made clear, "is contrary to no religion. Our people are free to embrace any faith."

Father Donovan passed word to Wang to tell the Catholics of Sung Shu Chen to devote their share of time to construction of the Confucian Memorial Shrine, since it violated no church principle. They obeyed.

Late one golden afternoon, as Father Donovan rode through the hills from Pin-Hu Kou, on the last leg to the mission at Lin Kiang, a human imitation of a bird call broke the almost audible quiet. It was in a deep valley, with browning hills soaring upward on every side. Wang Yun Chang recognized the call. "It is the robbers' lookout," he whispered to the padre. "He is hidden somewhere on these mountains and he is calling to his fellows. This time we shall be taken."

"Keep riding," Father Donovan told him quietly.

Suddenly a lone horseman on a fast pony broke from a

thicket and spurred down the hillside. He waved a rifle and the mountains echoed his threatening cries. From other places in the hills—from behind trees and great boulders—other ragged highwaymen thundered down on the missioner and his frightened assistant.

Presently the travellers sat their stubby little mounts within a circle of chattering brigands. Some of the robbers, with the naive curiosity of their race—it happened all the time in remote hamlets and villages—edged forward to stare at Father Donovan and comment openly on his strange features. They had never seen a white man before.

Father Donovan and poor Wang were herded down the valley to a great cave in the rocks, before the robber chief. Around the chief were more of the band, all armed, all grimy and ragged. The leader looked a long time at the priest in silence. He turned and fixed a hardened stare on the group that had brought the prisoners to him. "We do not stop this man," he said coldly. "He is the new *Shen Fu* from Lin Kiang." He turned back to Father Donovan, and apologized for his men. "Go your way," he said. "My men will not trouble you again."

In 1935, Father Donovan built a playground for children in Lin Kiang Mission—see-saws, swings and an outdoor gymnasium. He told Kate in one of his letters that he was astonished to find children on the swings and slides before sun-up each morning. "They get here at the most ungodly hours," the letter said, "and they stay until sundown." He bought a shelter for the homeless beggars of the town and supplied fuel to keep them warm. Food was scarce and he gave them rice and sorghum. Pagan merchants in the town were impressed by this gesture of the "foreign devil" to

their own poor whom they had neglected. Some sent dona-
tions of grain. They bowed and smiled to Father Donovan
when they met him in the streets.

On February 5, 1936, a band of robbers captured Father
Clarence Burns of the Tung Hua Mission in Manchukuo
after they had decoyed him with a false sick call. They held
him in the mountains, for ten months, dodging pursuing
details of soldiers. He staggered out of the hills one day
in November, bearded and emaciated. The robbers had
voted to kill him, since no ransom had been paid and the
soldiers were closing in, but at the last moment they had
turned him loose and vanished into the deep forests. Father
Burns was back on his legs again within a few weeks.

In August, 1937, Monsignor Lane assigned Father
Donovan to the mission at Hopei, across the river Hun
from the Maryknoll center at Fushun. A delegation of the
Lin Kiang parish elders came to Father Donovan just
before his departure to thank him for his works in the
community. "We are not men of fine words, Shen Fu,"
the spokesman told him, "but it is our wish that you know
that when you leave Lin Kiang you take some part of our
hearts with you." Father Donovan was touched. That night
he started down the Yalu toward his new post. He travelled
by what the natives called "the wind boat," a kind of sea
sled blown by an airplane propeller that skimmed the shal-
lows where an under-water propeller would snag.

Two months later, on the night of October 5, twilight
smudged the Hopei horizon and blurred the outlines of
trees and mountains. The chapel bell sounded in the sharp
air and shuffling feet whispered on the ground as parishioners moved toward the church. Children's cries were almost

cricket-like in their clarity in the freezing air. Across the river in Fushun, town lights bobbed and twinkled. In the distance, the mountains retreated slowly with the coming of dark.

Old Lao Kao was at work in the mission garden. He muttered when a stranger interrupted him to beg for medicine. "It is not the time for distribution of medicines," old Lao told him grumpily. The stranger hesitated, moved toward the chapel. He paused in the doorway. Inside candles burned steadily at the altar and the sweet Chinese chanting—it was the second decade of the Rosary—enriched the crepuscular quiet. The stranger started quietly toward the altar. Veronica Marie, a Maryknoll Sister, barely looked up from her beads. She thought it was extraordinary for a parishioner to approach the altar during a service.

The ragged stranger seemed a little bewildered by the candle-light and the soft chant. He leaned forward, plucked at Father Donovan's surplice, and held up a folded piece of paper. By this time, heads had lifted uneasily all through the congregation and the chant seemed to falter. Father Donovan, aware of the distraction, gently took the stranger's arm and led him into the little chamber off the altar, the sacristy. The chant resumed its even flow again.

In the little room off the altar, Francis Liu, a boy of seventeen who studied in the mission school, was fanning charcoal for the incense burner. The stranger pulled a clumsy revolver from his rags and covered the boy and the priest. He spoke in a hoarse whisper. He said, "Outside we are many. You are few and there are many women. We will destroy you." He motioned the boy and the priest toward the door leading into the mission yard. Father Donovan nodded quietly to Francis Liu. He wrapped his surplice and cassock about him and led the way.

Outside, old Lao straightened painfully from his garden task. The stranger thrust at him, with his free hand, the paper he had offered to Father Donovan at the altar. He said, "Give this to the foreign devils' chief when we have gone." Old Lao took the paper with trembling fingers. His rheumy old eyes were fixed on the revolver. A second stranger came through the gate with a horse-pistol in his grip. He and his companion shoved their captives down the garden path toward the gate, and out into the growing dark. They headed toward the mountains.

Old Lao screamed for Pai the house-boy. "Bandits," he shrilled. "Bandits, Pai. They have taken the Shen Fu." He thrust into Pai's hand the paper the bush rangers had left. He told him to hurry to the police station with it, to spread the alarm. When the police came to hear old Lao's excitable account of the kidnapping, the mountains were already muffled in utter darkness. The night wind was keening. Lanterns bobbed in the blackness and the first searching party, armed with rifles, moved toward the hills.

When Monsignor Lane got word of the incident across the bridge at Fushun he started a messenger to Mukden to ask help of John Davies, acting American Consul. A message flashed across the Pacific by wireless and across the United States to Maryknoll at Ossining in New York: "Bandits entered Fushun-Hopei parish chapel at 6 P.M. Took Donovan. (signed) Lane."

Father Donovan and Francis Liu were hurried up stony paths, under sparkling stars, by their captors. This was the

Season-of-Frost-Descent by the Manchukuo almanac and the night was sharply cold. The prisoners were not dressed for it. Father Donovan still wore only his thin cassock and he was hatless. He had no gloves. After an hour, the party turned off the path and plunged into the woods. The bush rangers seemed to know their way by instinct. They led the prisoners toward a rude thatched shelter where lanterns showed a faint light.

The band's chief, it turned out, was Swang Shan, a local boy who had made no good, so to speak. He was broad, flat-faced, short, like all his fellows, swathed in several thicknesses of coating, several layers of trousers. The shelter was stuffy with the odor of wet dog. Swang Shan studied the little priest. He fingered Father Donovan's spectacles and inspected the figure before him by the yellow lamp glow. He told Father Donovan he would be held until the other missioners sent $50,000 in American money.

"You waste your time, Swang Shan," Father Donovan told him. "My Church spends no money for ransom."

Swang Shan took this as bluff. He said, "We shall get $50,000, or we shall have to choke you and leave your body for the wolves."

"*Sui pien*," the little padre murmured. It was the native phrase for, "Have it your way."

The robber band moved by night, constantly shifting to throw off pursuit. They holed up by day, with lookouts posted on nearby crests to watch all approaches. Father Donovan noticed that most of the men were in their late 'teens, apparently farm boys from the district who decided they could make a better living by looting and kidnapping than by working the soil. They were not particularly hostile. When they found he could not stomach the ordinary mess they cooked for themselves they managed to create a kind of flour dumpling or to steal eggs for his diet.

They took his trousers and gave him a pair of their own—tattered, threadbare cotton, stiff with grease and grime. On the other hand, they gave him a cotton-padded jacket to protect him from the cold. They rather admired his unfailing grin and his easy laughter, though after a few days on the trail his feet puffed and blistered, and he limped painfully among them. In this band, only Swang Shan rode. They were a poor lot, even as Manchukuoan robbers go. They were on the move eleven days before they came to a permanent hideout in the deep woods. From this point they sent Francis Liu out with a second ransom note. Two of the gang showed the boy the way back.

Francis Liu turned up in the village of Ta-Hu-Tun, footsore and bleeding, on October 18, and turned over the second ransom note. Monsignor Lane and the other missioners eagerly heard his story. When he had finished they were somewhat relieved. It seemed, then, as though Swang Shan had acted with some degree of kindness toward Father Donovan and that he might turn the little padre out when he was convinced there would be no ransom. After all, Father Burns had been held ten months and had come back all right.

The missioners wrote an appeal to Swang Shan. "You ask this money," their letter said, "of a religious society which gives all it has to the poor and to old men and women who are helpless. It is difficult for us to understand why you have taken Father Donovan. He left his parents, his home and his country to come to your country to do good for the poor, such as yourselves."

The native delegation sent into the mountains with this letter came back empty-handed. They had not seen Father Donovan but members of the band had naively pointed out that Father Donovan was an American. In America, the robbers had heard, was a district called California. In California was Old Gold Mountain where any man might pick himself a pan of gold that would easily come to the amount of the ransom. Let the missioners send some of this gold and Father Donovan would be freed. To the robbers, it was as simple as that.

The months went by. Rumors drifted in from remote villages that Father Donovan had passed with the robber band. Several times word came through that he had been released in the mountains and was trekking missionward again. All these rumors were false. Protestant missioners had helped in the search. They made inquiries at their mountain outposts. They had prayed as fervently for Father Donovan as had the men and the Sisters of Maryknoll. The American consul had urged the Manchukuoan authorities to enlarge the search. Nothing came of all this.

On February 11, 1938, Monsignor Lane heard from John Davies. A body had been found in the snow at the foot of a mountain in Huai-Jen, some sixty miles or more from the mission center. It had not been identified. Would Monsignor Lane send a priest to fly to Huai-Jen with Ray Ludden of the consulate?

Next morning—it was Sunday—Ray Ludden and Father Tom Quirk, a Maryknoll missioner from Portsmouth,

N. H., landed in Huai-Jen. Soldiers and wide-eyed natives muffled in padded garments against the knifing wind followed them to a little compound where the body lay. One of the elders said that Fu Sheng, a forest freebooter, had dropped word at an inn the day before that he had come across it at the foot of the mountain. Soldiers had brought it back into the village.

Father Quirk recognized the remnants of the cassock, the broken spectacles, but not the features. This was not the kid from McKeesport as he had known him. The toes were frozen. The cotton-padded jacket and the cloth slippers had been ripped to tatters by wolves. The temple was bruised and the neck showed the mark of the strangling-rope.

The body was brought back to Hopei. Old Lao, and Francis Liu the house-boy, old Chinese men and women who had loved him, wept when the Laughing Father, as they knew him, started home. Doctor Leggate, the Scotch Presbyterian missioner said, after the departure, "I shall always be proud that I knew him. I shall always think of him as one who followed the Master closely."

Father Donovan sleeps on the Knoll. Mary Donovan saw him put to rest there. There were no tears. She merely stared at the coffin, raised her eyes toward Heaven.

"God's will be done," she murmured brokenly.

VII

Antu Christmas

THE WILDERNESS TRAIL to Antu is dangerous. It stretches
through tremendous forests where wolves, bears, wild boars
and wildcats have their lairs. It ranges up and down fabulous *Lao Pai San* or Old White Mountain. It winds around
the *T'ien Che*, a great crater lake of which the Manchus
speak, in awe, as Heaven's Pond. This lake is supposed to
be the dwelling place of the grandfather of all dragons.
The fish in its icy blue waters, a strange variety with spike-
like scales, are, according to local superstition poisonous
to humans. The Manchus seldom go near it, even though
the region yields valuable falcon feathers and ginseng,
both highly prized as native medicines.

Father Joseph Sweeney and Father Francis Bridge were
not bothered by local superstitions, but they knew the trail
might well be a Winter death trap. Just one year before,
in December, 1929, Father Sweeney had covered only 200
miles of the journey from Fushun to Lin Kiang, a somewhat less formidable trail when Doctor Hoh, his native
assistant, had died in the bitter cold. Father Sweeney bore
Dr. Hoh on their sled to the next inn, had a coffin made,
and took him back, alone. There had been no heroics about

it. Father Sweeney's report to the home Knoll barely mentioned it in passing.

Antu lies just under the Siberian border, some 450 miles upcountry from the mission center at Fushun. Father Sweeney had heard vague native rumors of a handful of Christians at Antu who had long before lost contact with the world outside. His idea was to bring Christmas to them. He estimated that a six weeks' start might give him some margin. He prepared for the trip as Commander Peary prepared for the polar dash, and looked pretty much as Peary did on the trail. He chose as companion Dr. Wong, who had replaced Dr. Hoh.

Father Sweeney had not counted on Father Bridge making the journey. Bridge had spent his childhood in the coal mines in Pennsylvania's Westmoreland Fields. He had been an A. E. F. sergeant in the first world war. Now fighting inevitable death from a painful disease, he stubbornly kept on at Fushun Mission. "I don't want to go home," he'd say. "I'd rather work and die in Manchuria." His superiors, who knew the spirit, allowed him to remain.

Just before Father Sweeney and Dr. Wong left their mission for Antu, Father Bridge showed up. He was muffled, as they were, in coat, trousers and cap of wolf-skin. Under this layer of fur he had sheep-wool secondary garments. Only his eyes and the top of his nose were visible in the frosty air. His feet were enormous in over-size boots and several strata of wool stockings. He was jubilant at the prospect of adventure. He had sent Barney Google, as he called his house-boy, back to the mission with Spark and Plug, his ponies. "I'm with you for Antu and a Merry

Christmas and a Happy New Year," he exulted. There was nothing Father Sweeney could do about it.

To awed natives Father Sweeney and Father Bridge looked—as indeed physically they were—like supermen. Father Sweeney was six feet, three inches high, Father Bridge six feet, two. In their furs they had monstrous proportions. Their mission kits were stowed on a native *kali*, rather large wooden sled with box-like chassis. They got the *kali* aboard the train at Fushun and made the first leg of their journey by rail to Tun-hua, the end of the line. This took them through dark, interminable Kirin Forest, haunt of Manchurian Robin Hoods and all manner of other predatory wild life.

At Tun-hua, they heard a German Benedictine monk maintained a mission on the forest's rim, some distance from the station. They started for it at noon. Screaming gales searched out open places in their parkas and blinded them with powdery snow. At intervals they stumbled, chest high, through enormous drifts that all but buried Dr. Wong. The glare off the snow, while the sun was high, created little islands of dark in their vision. When this became unbearable they held one hand on the sled ropes and covered their eyes with the fur mitts. There were, of necessity, frequent rests. Father Bridge's breath came hard. He'd turn his head away, so the others might not see him fight for air.

Native policemen stopped the party three times on the trail to the forest mission. They were inclined to disbelieve it was actually trying for Antu in what they called the Great-Snow-Month. Finally convinced this was the idea, they tried to talk the missioners out of it, but Father Sweeney and Father Bridge quietly explained it was something they *had* to do. The little policemen marvelled at these mad foreign giants, and waved them on.

At ten o'clock that night, all limbs acreak, Father Bridge made out a cross against the brilliant low-hung stars. The party floundered toward it. It was dark. Wind tried to tear the low mud shack free from the drifts. Half-frozen, Father Bridge pounded stiffly at the gate. He and Father Sweeney called hoarsely to the inmates. For ten minutes there was no answer. The wind snatched the cries from their numbed lips and tore them into insignificant syllables. The gate-thumping was barely audible above the gale.

Finally, though, the mission door opened. A startled Manchu boy gaped sleepily from behind a guttering lantern at the towering, snow-covered visitors. He slammed the door shut hastily and bolted it from inside. Father Bridge broke into sudden laughter and fur a moment Father Sweeney thought hysteria crouched behind the outburst. "No use," Father Bridge bellowed, "to every wise house-boy we can only be highwaymen. I'll try to reach the padre with Latin." He edged closer to the mission door. He roared in Latin, "Please open that gate before Christmas. We're American missioners from Fushun."

The door opened again. Behind the lantern, this time, stood the Benedictine monk, a little man with a great beard. The light shone on his pink, bald head. Blue eyes, somewhat myopic, stared at the Maryknoll men from behind thick lenses. The little man had a big voice. He threw the door wide and the travellers pushed through, shaking the snow from their parka and shoulders. The room was pleasantly warm. The *k'ang*—the native stove bed—was heated and the visitors, rid of outer garments, stretched on it to bake the stiffness from their bones.

In the lantern's light, the priests saw a low native table cluttered with books and papers. Father Liborius Morgenschweis, the Benedictine, apologized for the scholarly disorder. "I am writing a Chinese-Korean dictionary for the missions," he explained in Latin. He seemed fascinated by the idea of a journey to carry Christmas to Antu, but, like the native trail policemen, he doubted if the party would get through. He stirred the frightened house-boy into making hot tea. The priests talked long past midnight, curled up on the re-stoked *k'angs* and plunged into subregions of slumber.

While the expedition rested two days with Father Morgenschweis, Father Bridge bought Mongolian ponies to pull the *kalis*. Antu, at this stage, lay more than 100 miles to the southeast, Fushun 550 miles southwest. Lin Kiang, nearest Maryknoll post, was at the Korean-Manchurian border, 300 miles south. The little Benedictine went a little way with the expedition, trying to the last moment to persuade the American padres to celebrate Christmas with him and his handful of parishioners. They thanked him, but pushed on. The goal was Christmas in Antu.

They walked, because even with fur covers in the *kali* box, limbs soon numbed in the intense cold. And they walked briskly. To stop was to invite frostbite and complete numbness. Twenty-five miles took them out of open country again and into tremendous forest. They moved like pygmies through the snow under trees that soared, in some cases, more than a hundred feet. Father Bridge seemed in

excellent health after the rest. Sight of the great trees
reminded him of schooldays back in the coal country and
he recited, so the forest echoed and re-echoed the words:
"This is the forest primeval . . ."

"The great forests of giant pine, spruce, oak, walnut
and elm," Father Sweeney remembers, "were, to us, inspir-
ingly beautiful. You caught the sense of something over-
whelmingly strong, but asleep under an immaculate man-
tle. There was cause for exultation in the knowledge that
no white men had ever passed this way before us. The
Christians were immigrants from Shantung."

Beyond the Kirin boundary line, the expedition to
Antu struck eastward. As the sun went down the second
night out, they saw a tiny cluster of mud dwellings
through the twilight. Snarling dogs, much like wolves,
barked at their approach and little fur-bundled men came
outdoors to stare at them. Their size excited lively communal debate. The little men and the village children
circled Father Sweeney and Father Bridge to observe their
height from different angles. This was like Barnum and
Bailey come to town. They had never seen white men before. They were especially fascinated by the missioners'
noses. Their own were mere buttons. The priests' noses,
normal enough where white men dwell, were monstrosities
to them.

That night the Antu Christmas expeditionary force slept
at the primitive inn in the wilderness. The one room that
was the entire establishment had rush lighting. It was heavy
and thick with smoke that seeped through cracks in the
k'angs that stretched along either wall. The natives were
conditioned to the smoke and their eyes remained wide in

undiminished wonder at the size of these strangers. Each newcomer, brought by eager messengers from outside, boldly approached the missioners to study their incredible proportions at close range. A few ventured to feel the noses. Father Bridge and Father Sweeney didn't mind, particularly. This experience was not altogether new.

After a hot supper, eaten on the brick-topped *k'angs*, the travellers stretched out to sleep—parallel with the inn walls. The slant-eyed boniface and his other guests—there were a few—slept with the top of their heads against the wall, but they could. Most of them were under five feet in height.

Father Bridge took sick through the night. Father Sweeney, staring up through the smoke-filled dark, heard him stifle sounds of pain. He nudged the soldier priest. He whispered, "Frank, we'll start back tomorrow. We'll pass Christmas in that German mission." Father Bridge lay quiet. Finally he said, "I don't want to seem tough about it, Joe, but tomorrow we'll do no such thing." He fished for his medical kit in the dark and fumbled for a little bottle of pain-killing pellets. He swallowed them. "Be okay in the morning, Joe," he assured Father Sweeney. "Goodnight."

Oddly enough he did seem improved when the inn stirred to life in half-dark before the wintry sunrise. He said, "I feel like the whole Notre Dame backfield. Don't get in my way, or try to stop me. It's on to Antu."

They were five days on the trail from the Benedictine's mission to Antu. On the third, they came out of the woods again into great areas cleared, quite obviously, both by the woodsman's axe and by great forest fires that had brought thousands of the towering pines and elms to charred stumps and ashes. Eventually they crossed a vast, snowy plain where the only trees that seemed to flourish were occasional clumps of deciduous pines. They encountered a few wayfarers but these, after their initial fright and astonishment, knew of no Catholics in, or near Antu. Worse than that, they had never heard of Christians, let alone Catholics. The expedition pushed on, nevertheless.

Early in the afternoon of the fourth day, the party topped a ridge and from this crest stared in breathless wonder at *Lao Pai San,* the Old White Mountain of Manchu legends. It had been a hard day. For the second time since they had put out of Tun-Hua, their *kali* had torn from its ropes and had dropped in splinters, into a yawning, snow-filled gorge so deep that its bottom was merely a black pit. This time, as on the first, their precious mission kits and their medicines had, fortunately, spilled in the snow on the trail and the Mongolian ponies had managed to save themselves from the death plunge.

In spite of these hardships and losses, the two Americans were lost in reverent thought over *Lao Pai San's* beauty. They could understand, at this moment, why this volcanic peak had bred so many native superstitions. From somewhere beneath this mountain, and under the ice-blue waters of Heaven's Pond, incidentally, flow the Yalu, Sungari and Tumen Rivers that carry freight to lower Manchuria, when Spring releases Winter's icy fingers from their throats. The missioners turned, at last, from contemplation of the mountain's beauty and turned from the Chang Pai mountain range toward Antu.

The expedition had been lucky. In spite of predictions

they had somehow kept clear of the robber bands in Chapei Forest though the woods swarmed with them. These latter-day blood-brothers of Robin of Nottinghamshire, are mostly descendants—or so the local stories go—of the great Nurhachu, founder of the Manchu Dynasty, who assembled the primitive hunters and woodsmen of upper Manchuria for the incredible trek that ended in Peking, with Nurhachu's kin on the Emperor's throne in the Middle Kingdom.

Anyway, a Divine hand seemed to be gently steering the Antu expedition clear of major harm and mischief. Dr. Wong, riding somewhat ahead of the *kali* the night before they approached Antu, suddenly came tearing back through the deep snow with his pony in a lather. He seemed agitated. "We must turn off from this next settlement," he babbled to the two priests. "The inn there is infested with highwaymen." Wong had stumbled into the inn, it turned out, but the armed band hadn't noticed. Guards and all were whirling giddily in top Heaven, sodden with opium. The priests were fatigued but they worked their way wearily around the settlement. They slept that night off the trail.

The sun was gone and the air crackled and snapped with cold well under 50 degrees below zero when Antu showed up in their sight the next night. It was December 23, 1930. Again they had floundered and gasped their way all day through man-high drifts and wind-blasted snow had picked their faces raw. They were on the verge of utter snow-blindness. They crossed the upper Sungari River on solid ice and drove under Antu's West Gate. Antu is a walled town and lookouts are perched along the walls to sight possible enemies—local hoop-de-doos break out in this region occasionally when the lads get bored—but it seems there were no guards this night.

The West Gate was locked, but scouting around the outer wall the expedition found a crude inn still open. Their stomping entry, as they shook the snow from their furs, stopped local inn gossips mid-phrase, so to speak. Here, as in earlier stops among primitives, the Americans' extraordinary height left the hometown talent agape. "It must have been the same when the Indians first saw Christopher Columbus," Father Sweeney's apt to say when he recounts it. When the inn's customers had had an eyeful, they rushed into the open to spread the word about the gigantic freaks who had materialized out of the night. The inn owner suddenly found his place packed to the doors.

Those who couldn't squeeze into the inn did the next best thing. They punched through the inn's parchment windows and stared over the heads of their fellow-townsmen for a peek, shrilly calling the Antu term for, "Holy Smoke!" From within the wall came a fussy little man, sharp-eyed and keen, and a bit on the pompous side. He was some kind of official. He shouldered his way through the excitedly chattering common people and stared at the priests a long time. At last he thought he had it figured out. "Russians," he told the neighbors confidently. "Long noses from Siberia. I have seen others like these."

Father Bridge politely corrected him. "Americans," he told the fussy little man in Mandarin. "We come from the Beautiful Land." The United States, it seems, are always the "Beautiful Land" to people on the steppes. Fact is, the appellation originated in the East through the accident that the Chinese character officially chosen to approximate the sound of its first syllable happens to mean "beautiful."

The fussy gentleman made a kind of stump speech about the Beautiful Land. "Americans," he said, in effect, "they are a great people. No flies on Americans." This is not a true translation, Father Sweeney would hasten to explain, but it carries the germ of the speech. It was much longer and pretty flowery, but that's typical of Oriental speeches. You talk your way around a block to cross a conversational crack one foot away.

Next morning, after a night on the inn's *k'ang*, the expedition entered the West Gate. The fussy little man, his confidence bolstered by further information from the Americans, proudly led them along narrow gutters through swarms of fellow-citizens and shrieking children. These, he declaimed, were Catholic priests, representatives of the Catholic Church. This didn't seem to mean much, so he tried to get the idea over in a simpler way. He said, "These foreigners walk the good road. Their church is the good road gate." The populace nodded, as if all got it, and crowded closer.

Father Sweeney and Father Bridge were bearded when they reached the inn, but they had washed and shaved when they got off the *k'angs* in the morning. They had been careful to scour the wooden wash basin with ashes and to use carbolic soap for lather. The basin was community property. Now, hemmed in by the hordes, the priests were clear-cheeked and ruddy. Antu, they noted, was a square city within square walls. It was protected by a medieval moat and its two main streets crossed in the town's center, each street end stopping dead at a gate.

The missioners recognized in drawn features and heavy-lidded eyes, all about them, the marks of opium smokers. They learned later that poppies are extensively cultivated outside Antu in the brief Summer, and that the seeds are made into the sticky gum that is Asia's curse. The local chief of police was eager to help. He begged the visitors to have dinner in his humble home—a mud-walled, grass thatched little place like most of the others in Antu—but they had to beg off. They explained they had come over difficult road to celebrate an important holy day. He tried to be helpful anyway, but like the rest of the townsfolk, knew of none of the Catholic immigrants from Shantung in Antu.

Father Sweeney looked at Father Bridge and Father Bridge looked back at Father Sweeney. It was heart-breaking, after the journey to bring Christmas to Antu, to find that the reports of forgotten Antu Christians were apparently myths, after all. Anyway, they decided to celebrate the Mass on their own. The inn wasn't a likely place for it. No privacy. Besides, it was not decent atmosphere for the Holy Sacrifice. At last they found an old couple in a one-room mud hut near the inn who seemed willing to rent their place for the service. This couple, pagans, moved into the noisy inn.

The rented room was about ten feet wide, fifteen feet long. The thatch ceiling was low. In one corner stood a mud stove that was weak on heat but generous with smoke. In a farther corner were two forty-gallon jugs of pickled Chinese cabbage, somewhat on the high side, and along one wall the traditional *k'ang*. An old hen had the run of the place and kept getting underfoot, grumpily uttering a sort of running commentary on the poor pickings. There was an aged, long-haired tomcat, too, which slept most of the time on the *k'ang*. Oddly enough, it made no passes at the grumpy hen, which astonished the Americans.

Father Bridge set the rickety table in place as an altar. Father Sweeney helped him. Still weary from their travels and not a little sore at heart over their failure to find the forgotten Christians to whom they had meant to bring Christmas, they finally dropped onto the *k'ang*. Joe Sweeney was a long way from Clark Street in New Britain, Conn.; Frank Bridge was a far cry from the little mine shack in the Westmoreland Fields, and the surroundings weren't the least bit like home on Christmas Eve, but they fell into deep sleep, just the same, with the decrepit tomcat purring a lullaby.

Father Bridge was first up, Christmas morning. He awakened Father Sweeney with a deep-throated version of "Adeste Fideles." He sang "The Star Spangled Banner," and Father Sweeney stood up and sleepily came to salute. When the anthem ended, Father Sweeney said, "The same to you, Sir, and many of them." The tomcat yawned. The gossipy old hen fluffed her feathers and started moving around, still complaining.

Father Sweeney served the first Mass ever celebrated in far-off Antu. Before he had quite finished, Dr. Wong pushed open the creaky cottage door. Four Catholics who had lived a full decade in Antu—they were some of the sought-for immigrants from south of the Great Wall— stood behind him. Tears ran down their withered cheeks at sight of the little altar and the vested giant priests towering in the candlelight. During the second Mass another Chinese Christian slipped into the room. He had heard of the missioners from the Beautiful Land as he passed by the inn. The room glowed in the candles' weak beams. Father Bridge cupped his hands around the chalice to prevent the Sacred Species from freezing. When the Mass was ended he sang again, in sheer exultation, and his voice was vibrant and rich:

"O, Little Child of Bethlehem . . ."

The simple hymn faded, and died in Antu's frozen air. Antu's little knot of Christians came to press the Shen Fu's hands in gratitude. One old woman murmured, "Father, come back to us again. Do not discard our souls."

Frank Bridge died in St. Mary's Hospital in San Francisco, three years later, in April, when Spring was at the windows. He was then thirty-eight. He had worked in the mines as a boy, in the Pittsburgh steel mills and with the A. E. F. in his youth, and had been ten years in the missions. He never forgot the first Christmas in frozen Antu. In brief respite from pain in the hospital he liked to tell about that day. He'd say: "I always thought the little room in Antu that morning was like the stable in Bethlehem, and that the worshippers were like the shepherds. I never knew a happier Christmas."

VIII

Monsignor Moonface

ON A SPRING AFTERNOON in 1915, Sister Grace Winifred's eighth-graders in St. Joseph's School in suburban New Rochelle pounded down the block and cut across lots, whooping and shouting—all but "Chink" Romaniello, class mischief-maker. The teacher dropped a magazine on the boy's desk. "Look through that," she told him tartly. "Maybe it will make you understand what we suffer for the likes of you." Outdoors shrillness gradually receded. The classroom clock reluctantly released the seconds. A half-hour later the teacher was ready to let the boy go. She returned the magazine—a copy of Maryknoll's "Field Afar," to her drawer. The boy lingered, inordinately pensive. "I think maybe I'll join the missions, Sister," he told her dreamily. The teacher sniffed. John Romaniello trudged downstairs and took the short cut to Fourth Street under greening sidewalk trees. He moved in a trance that could have been nothing more than a sudden attack of Spring fever.

Fate must laugh, sometimes, at her own whimsy in patterning human destinies. Today an outstanding figure in

139

ancient Kweilin, a former dwelling place of Chinese Emperors, is "Monsignor Moonface," a broad smiling man with receding dark hair whose friendly eyes shine through silver spectacles. Chinese moppets leap up from play in congested Kweilin's streets to shrill greeting as he comes by. Merchants bow and call dignified salutation from shop doorways and from passing rickshas. Perspiring coolies, bent under incredible loads, grin as they approach him and speak their affection in high-pitched, firecracker phrases. "Monsignor Moonface," as the natives fondly call him, is a Kweilin favorite. To them he is the foreigner who stayed with the city's poor and unsheltered, who fed and clothed them after the soldiers of Japan had reduced their city to mounds of rubble filled with dead and dying.

This is Sister Grace Winifred's plaguey Romaniello boy, twenty-eight years later.

John Romaniello was born on September 12, 1900, in rural Avigliona, near Potenza, east of Naples. He was one of thirteen children. His father, Angelo Romaniello, was a shepherd, his mother, Angela, a peasant girl. The family came steerage to the United States in 1906. Angelo Romaniello worked as a laborer, sometimes in the streets, sometimes as a gravedigger in the Beechwood Cemetery in New Rochelle. Finally, he decided on the gravedigger career and worked at it for more than thirty-three years. Of his children, born to hardship and want, only two survived, Vito who became an ice peddler and John, who'd put his hand to anything that came along. Angela Romaniello has been dead many years. Angelo is seventy-eight, a little bent and withered, but he grows watery-eyed with pride when anyone mentions Monsignor John.

In boyhood, John Romaniello held no extraordinary promise. He was, if anything, rather slow in class. At twelve he caddied for the golfers at Wykagyl. When there were no caddying jobs he swam lazily in Long Island Sound off Hudson Beach Park with other kids, or went to the movies. When Vito got the ice route in Pelham, John rode the truck with him, making deliveries. Priesthood was not in his early dreams, not until Sister Grace Winifred kept him in after class that Spring day. Her sniff of disbelief, she willingly concedes now, was unjustified and she's apt to get teary-eyed over her letters from Kweilin. They still come. "John wasn't really a bad boy," she hastens to explain in discussing the incident that turned him toward the missions. "Just a little wild."

There were thirteen years' schooling after the eighth grade incident before Father John Romaniello, late on the afternoon of September 9, 1928, left the Seminary on Sunset Hill in Ossining, headed for South China and the missions. He had scarcely set foot outside New York State before, and his first letters home as he stopped in St. Louis, at the Grand Canyon, San Francisco and Seattle were filled with a naive wonder at the country's vastness and beauties. He mailed back copies of dining car and hotel menus on this trip and when the President Pierce bore him deep into the Pacific, kept a day-by-day account of new wonders. In Fourth Street, Papa Romaniello eagerly heard all the details then went among his neighbors to relate them, over and over again. Fourth Street followed John Romaniello clear into South China.

The young missioner was a faithful correspondent. Sometimes the letters betrayed a cut of homesickness, but mostly they maintained the naive outlook. They told of Cantonese instruction at Pingnam under Father Bernard Meyer. "From five o'clock in the morning, until long after dark," one letter related, "I keep at it, and sometimes I wonder whether I shall ever really conquer it." Father Romaniello's tutor taught him to use chopsticks, so that he might not lose face when he sat down to his first family meal in China, drilled him in native habits and customs, took him on long mountain treks to outpost missions.

His letters told of Chinese curiosity about Americans. A scholarly Chinese gentleman politely stopped him in Pingnam one morning and to the young missioner's astonishment held up a dog-eared copy of *The Boston Post*.

"Is this from your country?" he wanted to know, and the priest said it was.

"Would the American gentleman deign to read it, please?" the scholarly Chinese asked.

No foreigner stops in the street in an inland Chinese city without attracting a crowd. Pretty soon Father Romaniello and the scholar were enclosed in a ring of curious men, women and children, six feet deep. Father Romaniello read the newspaper's name and some of the headlines. The crowd tittered at the unfamiliar syllable. Gradually the titters grew to loud laughter. The Chinese were amused. The scholarly gentleman turned to them. "You see," he told them, "it is a strange language, not at all like Chinese, not a single word." Father Romaniello, somewhat embarrassed, moved off, and the crowd kept trying out the strange

American words. "Bo-si-Tun" the urchins shrieked. "Bo-si-Tun." They found the sound highly diverting.

Letters home told of the narrow, crooked streets in Pingnam, described the miserable little shops that were hardly shops at all. They described the shrill conversation that keeps the average thoroughfare in China in constant bedlam, told of the ancient wall around the city, and lapsed into nostalgia in a brief account of the homesickness that clutched the heart at sight of an American flag over the Standard Oil office in Wuchow. Father Romaniello often wandered by the river and came back with ample copy about the junks, the sampans and the urchin-cluttered houseboats he had seen. The family in Fourth Street got a stirring account of his first trip on a junk. This told of the Chinese patience when boats were hours late, as they almost always were, and how the passengers didn't seem to mind when the junk put in for an unscheduled stop at a landing and took on a cargo of pigs to share the deck with them.

In July, 1929, Father Meyer took the new man on his first long outside mission journey. He set an appalling pace. Father Romaniello's feet blistered as he loped along stony mountain paths, trotted on narrow walks in the rice fields, waded streams, plodded through tremendous downpours. "I'm afraid I'm a bit soft," the letters said, "but sooner or later my feet will harden and my leg muscles will get used to it." The letters still carried ample detail about the Chinese farmers' cheerful greetings, told about cricket-sized Chinese boys bullying the tremendous water buffaloes, so common for all heavy work in South China.

In August the dispensary at Pingnam got into full swing.

Father Romaniello had to overcome the natural revulsion that attacks every new missioner when he first looks upon, and handles, exaggerated infections. He was amused by Chinese names for the various medicines. They called tincture of iodine, "iodine wine," and when they smelled disinfectant referred to it as, "the stinking water." The mysteries of the Western Pharmacopoeia excited their natural curiosity. They would accept almost any kind of medicine any time, in a strictly experimental way. Father Romaniello had to teach them not to eat the thermometer. At first new patients thought the idea was to crunch this foreign medicine and get it down some way. They were always willing to try anything new.

In September a modern blimp soared over Pingnam on global tour. Chinese craned their necks and burst into excitable discussion of this sky monster. Father Romaniello was impressed, almost, but not quite as much as they were. He thought wistfully that if he could get aboard he'd be back in Fourth Street in a few days, and the thought went into a letter. Around this time, though, homesickness had begun to wear off. There was too much to do, too many things to learn and see, for a man to let his thoughts dwell forever on New Rochelle. Within eighteen months the first visible signs of the true missioner had developed.

Early in 1930, Father Meyer decided his curate was ready to go into a new field on his own. He assigned Father Romaniello to Watlam. A Chinese tax bureau had the house when the new pastor reached it. The officials promised to leave, but press of business had kept them over. The building was untidy, white ants had hollowed out many of the beams, walls and floors were inches deep in grime.

Finally the tax officials moved, but to Father Romaniello's distress, the departing tenants meticulously pulled out all electric wires. It seems this is a Chinese tradition, too. Electric wires are part of the tenant's fixtures. When he moves, the wires move with him.

Father Romaniello got on his hands and knees, because he had no servants, not even the customary house-boy, and scrubbed the floor clean. The first night was extremely cold and he had no bedding. He turned in, shivering, wearing all his street clothes including his overcoat and hat. He took off only his shoes. All in all, it was a rather unhappy night. He had been a dinner guest—at a native Christian's home in Watlam and his eyes had all but popped at some of the weird dishes. To a man trained pretty much on macaroni, spaghetti, ravioli and on American cooking, they were hard to take, but Father Meyer had sternly warned him that to refuse food in a Chinese home is to run grave risk of giving offense. Father Romaniello got it all down, but not without serious misgivings. He had smiled through it all and had murmured the polite phrases he had learned, but something like panic overtook him after he had bowed himself out. Lying on the bare floor in the unlighted mission, he stared up in the dark and wondered if he would survive.

He did, even though he got much more than he bargained for. Only a few weeks after he arrived at Watlam the city was besieged in a civil war. For nearly two months it held out. During that time food almost ran out. The city was shelled, one shell passing through one of the mission buildings. During this time Father John cared for wounded soldiers and civilians, and this so successfully that the soldiers would trust no treatments but his. He gained much face, though he was in constant danger. Eventually, a relief army came to save the besieged. Lacking food, money and medicine, Father Romaniello started overland for Wuchow through the enemy lines. He had a military pass from the victorious army which gave him the high sounding title of "chief chaplain" and "army doctor." He saved several officers when their bus got stuck in the mud by showing them how to get it out. Shortly afterwards guerillas appeared but the bus made off in safety. He arrived in Wuchow to find the pastor absent, no food in the house, no money. He had to borrow money to eat. Then, using his pass, he went to Pingnam for medicines and while there ran into another battle. Later he escorted wounded soldiers from both sides to the military hospital in Wuchow. In all this fuss of battle he became quite acclimated to gunfire.

Little by little, partly because of the Romaniello smile and because the new missioner was generous, Watlam Chinese came to the station to hear him talk about the "Lord of Heaven Doctrine," which was their name for the Catholic Religion. Sometimes it was the missioner's possessions that brought them over his threshold. His typewriter, for example, fascinated them. They would stand over his shoulder and murmur as each tap of the key left a symbol on paper. At their request he wrote their names in English. They would hurry into the street with these slips and Father Romaniello would see them haranguing groups of their fellows as they displayed the prize.

The women were especially eager for the missioner's old newspapers, which they used for wallpaper. When Father Romaniello had finished his copy of the *New Rochelle*

Standard, The New York Times and the Catholic publications, he distributed them. The women bore them off in high excitement. Later, when Father Romaniello entered the homes of some of these women, he could sit and read on the wall the stale news he had digested months before. The mission victrola seldom had a breathing spell. Chinese gathered outside the house in whispering groups, enthralled by its hoarse and rather cracked versions of "Little Grey Home In The West," "She's Only A Bird In A Gilded Cage," and other plaintive melodies, which somehow soothed them, though they prefer their own music in shrill quarter tones. They liked Gilbert and Sullivan, too.

Father Romaniello left Watlam for Kweilin in October, 1930. By this time he was steeped in work, and much of his Western strangeness had worn off. He had to learn the Mandarin dialect to get along in the new post, but this came much easier than Cantonese, because he had caught and mastered the trick of inflection which gives different meanings to the same word. Dr. Brown, the Baptist missioner in Kweilin, was friendly. Father Romaniello was a guest in his home soon after he reached the city, and a letter to Fourth Street told ecstatically how much he had appreciated Mrs. Brown's home-made ice cream. It had been two years since Father Romaniello had tasted ice cream.

Kweilin's beauty thrilled him. Against the western sky, huge limestone monoliths, fantastically shaped, were something a man could dream on. These jagged mountain formations, peculiar to Kwangsi Province, took on a weird quality at twilight. They reminded Father Romaniello, somehow, of his brief visit to Grand Canyon. Declining

sun colored their outer plains in incredibly beautiful
golden and rose shades, then deftly changed to purple.
The receding, or depressed plains, meanwhile, filled with
dusky shadow. The district was rich in ancient banyan
trees and the sun, rising or setting, gilded watery rice
fields. Solitary Mountain was a nightmare in technicolor
and to the South, Tooth Of The Moon soared in picturesque
grandeur to the lovely sky. It was a strange setting for the
boy from Fourth Street, but he loved it.

The mission was an ancient brick mansion, a little moss-
grown, somewhat decayed, but basically sound. Father
Romaniello called it The Ruined Palace. He was a little
puzzled, then bewildered, at first, because he could hire no
house servants for the place. Men and boys alike murmured
polite refusal when jobs were offered, though they were
extremely friendly. Father Romaniello tried to figure it
out, but got nowhere, and patiently did his own house-
cleaning. He was his own chef, too, working with a Boston
Cook Book spread before him. As weeks went by the
problem became acute. It was almost impossible to attend
to mission duties and to all the housework, too.

One day a Kweilin gentleman came out with the secret.
"The House in West Alley," he told the missioner, earnestly, "is haunted, and has been, for many years. Evil
shades walk in it, Lord of Heaven Man, and you would do
well to set up your mission elsewhere." According to local
legend, it turned out, a rich Chinese merchant prince had
lived in the house in West Alley, and with him a retinue
of servants. One of these, a lovely girl from Yungfu, the
"City of Eternal Happiness," which lies 40 miles outside
Kweilin, hanged herself to a rafter there one night for love

of her master. It was her restless spirit that roamed the
place. Merchants and children would stop the missioner in
the streets to ask, "Has the Lord of Heaven Man seen the
Spirit? Has she disturbed his sleep?" Eventually, when
they were assured the girl ghost must have left, Father
Romaniello acquired a service staff. He named his grinning
house-boy Sam Weller.

Local artisans scrubbed down the walls of The Ruined
Palace, swept away the cobwebs, whitewashed the interior
and, at the missioner's direction, built shelves and tables.
The place was dark, but Father Romaniello had windows
cut in the wall. These faced the old garden. The haunted
house now offered a fair degree of comfort. The parlor
was furnished with a table, an oil lamp, a stand for the
victrola, two hard chairs and one comfortable rocker. When
curates came to help, later, Father Romaniello made it a
rule that no man could set in the rocker until the day's
chores were ended. He found rocking too conducive to doz-
ing. When the northwinds blew, at night, they sometimes
worked in through the cracks. Father Romaniello wore a
heavy bathrobe around the house, even slept in it when the
winds had a frosty nip. At that, he was better off than most
of the poorer natives. From his windows he could see them,
wrapped from head to foot in burlap, wearing even burlap
for boots, walking head down against the gale.

In December, 1932, Father Romaniello celebrated his
fifth Christmas away from home. Christmas had been a
warm and joyous holiday back in Fourth Street. Here he
had only fourteen Chinese Christians at the Mass at which
he preached in Mandarin. Gifts were late coming from the
United States (in 1931, his Christmas package of tobacco,

canned fruits and dry macaroni and spaghetti did not
arrive until May), but Dr. Brown, the Baptist minister
and Mrs. Brown, sent over a box of nuts and a box of
candy. Still, Fourth Street had not really forgotten. There
were neighborhood bridge and block parties to raise funds
for the Kweilin Mission and enough money came through
to pay for painting the haunted house and for a better
kitchen.

Father Romaniello made his first trip over the mountains in January, 1933, to the mission of Tu Yang Ch'ao
in The Valley of The Earth-Nourishing Channel to visit
the Yaus, a mysterious aboriginal tribe who bear the same
relationship to the Chinese as American Indians do to us.
The Yaus live in the mountains altogether apart from the
Chinese of Kwangsi. They have no written language of
their own and their dress is considerably different from
the Chinese costume. They wear ceremonial conical straw
hats almost two feet high, go in for leggings that look
somewhat like the buckskins of Western Indian tribes and
their women spend years embroidering and beading their
marriage costumes. After marriage these garments are
worn only on special festive occasions. The missioners
found some 300 Yaus who had been converted by French
priests. On this trip, high in the jagged limestone formations, Father Romaniello trudged through the first snow
he had seen in five years. He had some July 1932 issues of
The New Yorker on this trip and tried to get an illusion
of warmth by reading the Summer ads. The temperature
in the mountains dropped to 24 degrees, which is decidedly
below the average for Kwangsi.

Father John's shock of dark black hair that had lifted in the breeze back on Sunset Hill was thinning rapidly. Kweilin shopkeepers had come to watch for the padre in his daily walks in the crowded thoroughfares. They bowed to him from their doorways. More and more Chinese came to the house in West Alley for religious instruction and this presented an expansion problem. Father Romaniello consulted a Kweilin carpenter on a new two-story building for the mission compound. Two stories? The architect didn't understand. He was sure one story would be safer. Besides, whoever gave the *Shen Fu* the notion that two-story houses are practical?

Father Romaniello dug out a copy of *The New Yorker* that had a color photograph of the Empire State Building. Kweilin's Stanford White stared at this a long time, shrugged, finally conceded the thing might work, after all. He got together a crew of fellow carpenters and construction started. It developed that the builder, though, had gotten the wrong impression from Father Romaniello's description of the Empire State Building. He went around the local tea houses telling his friends that in New York the Catholic Cathedral was a quarter-mile high—much higher, even, than Tooth of the Moon, out there on the skyline. He borrowed *The New Yorker* to prove it and the natives came to connect Father Romaniello with the building of the Fifth Avenue skyscraper. It gave him added face, so to speak, though he didn't need it. His face had rounded so that he had already become known as the "Moon-faced Lord of Heaven Man." His face, darkened by ardent South China sun, looked somewhat Chinese and he was sometimes mistaken for a native.

The mission had picked up, as sideline, the task of measuring Kweilin's rainfall for the Chinese Government's flood control bureau. The return from this was enough to pay the mission cook. Contributions from home and from the Society went into the purchase of a miniature motion picture projector, which drew additional visitors. The Chinese were fascinated by the "lightning shows," particularly by Charlie Chaplin films. Peasants from villages outside Kweilin were awed by them. Around this time Father Romaniello taught English to Chinese soldiers in Kweilin. Later, he was invited to teach English to advanced students in Kwangsi Medical College. He used doctrinal books for practical English, the only medium available.

After eight years in the field, Father Romaniello returned to the United States on furlough. There were feasts and celebrations in Fourth Street. Papa Romaniello got about amazingly, dragging home old friends and old cronies to have them see with their own eyes this son, this Father John, who had come back over 10,000 miles of land and sea. "Behold," he would tell them. "Listen to the adventures he has had among strange peoples in that strange land." Papa Romaniello was extraordinarily proud. So was Sister Grace Winifred. The dreamy-eyed boy who had stumbled from her room that distant Spring day was a laughing, erudite missioner, now. She loved to hear stories about his Chinese parishioners. She had come to think that a Divine Hand had prompted her to drop the "Field Afar" on his desk in the hushed classroom that afternoon in 1915. Twenty-one years had elapsed between that hour and the hour of his return from the far field.

When he left her, the teacher sniffed—but this time she sniffed back tears of joy.

2

Father Romaniello looked on China's shore again on August 26, 1937, this time from the decks of the Empress of Canada. Now he stared gloomily at a China invaded. He wrote home:

"We cannot enter Shanghai. It is a city in flames. The ship is anchored seven miles off shore. We have been here almost forty hours, and from this deck we have seen the war. At night we see the flares from the big guns and hear the roar of cannon.

"There are now on this ship three thousand people and every foot of space is used for sleeping. They are refugees from the city. Last night passengers volunteered to peel potatoes. I joined this group.

"This morning we could not say Mass. There was no room. People are milling all about me. The children seem oblivious of all that is happening. Five small boys are playing soldier on deck."

This was merely a preview of what lay ahead for the pastor of Kweilin Mission. He was to perform near miracles as Japanese hordes and their bombers crept down the coast, sowing death among the brave but ill-equipped Chinese.

In June, 1938, word came from Maryknoll in New York that Father Romaniello had been designated Prefect Apostolic of Kweilin. Meanwhile, Kweilin had come under Japanese aerial bombardment. Almost every day now the

missioners and their charges ran at least once for the limestone caves outside the city. These caves were natural bomb
shelters. Some were small and held only a few persons,
others were great caverns with room for thousands.
Acknowledging the message announcing his appointment
as Prefect, Father Romaniello wrote home, "As I stood
reading it the explosions got rather close. I found such
accompaniment a distraction. Father Greene and I ambled
off to the hills to enjoy Nature's peaceful quiet. I finished
reading it there."

By September, Kwangsi Province rocked under bomb
impact, day and night. The Japanese had little opposition.
They swooped just above the rooftops to get at their targets.
Bombs dropped in market places where Chinese congre-
gated in large numbers. The Chinese Kweilin airfield just
outside the city was a frequent objective, but this was one
of the only military targets in the district. In October,
Maryknoll's Kweilin compound was stampeded by an endless stream of unfortunates. Some had been bombed out
of Fukien, Kiangsi, Hunan and Chekiang provinces. Tens
of thousands had left ruined cities with little more than
the rags on their back. Families had scattered. Food was
unavailable. Thousands fell in the road.

Father Romaniello, his assistants and the Maryknoll
Sisters, worked among these refugees with lumps in their
throats. They had seen hardship and human suffering before, but nothing matched this. Some of the men and
women were weak skeletons who had eaten bark from trees
along the road. Men, women and children had hungrily
devoured grass when they reached districts which the
bombs had not burned over. Some were the wealthy of

North China in silks and well supplied with money, but their sufferings seemed no less severe. The almost lifeless moppets were pitifully swollen from insufficient diet. A young Chinese mother, already wrinkled and hallow-cheeked, gulped her rice in the compound and told how she had tied her children to a tree off the road while she searched and begged for something to give them. "They were too weak to go with me," she explained.

A scholarly Chinese gentleman who lost all his fortune in the bombing of Hunan had seen mothers, exhausted, sink in the road with children in their arms. Hungry tides swept around them, desperately set on making Kweilin. One mother lay dead in the road, her rigid arms holding a skeleton infant that whimpered and blubbered, until some-one lifted it from her arms and carried it along. In this ghastly procession there were many wounded—men and women lacking an arm or a foot, covering league after league with gangrene slowly rotting the injured limbs. Coolies carried some of the wounded on their backs. There were shrapnel cases, children torn by machine-gun bullets. Old people, overcome by hunger and by unaccustomed travel in the hurrying swarms lay dead everywhere along the path of flight. Their bodies were pushed off the high-way to let the living pass.

Bombs rained steadily on Kweilin, and it became rou-tine for Father Romaniello and his men to break the rice lines and take to the caves. He sent to other districts for more help, until he had nine priests, and several Mary-knoll Sisters working with him. By the end of 1938, Kwei-lin mission was handling more than 10,000 refugees each month; feeding the hungry, caring for the wounded, gathering in babies and older children whose parents had died in the flight from the bombed provinces, or who had been torn from their mothers in the hungry march on Kweilin. He begged for rice and more rice, long after his own mission funds were exhausted. With the help of relief organizations he managed, somehow, to keep the multitudes alive.

In the midst of all this, on December 29, 1938, Kweilin had its worst raid. That day Japanese bombs destroyed more than 1,000 homes in the city. Smoke and flame hovered over it for days.

Some nights the press of refugees was too much for the mission. Hundreds unable to enter lay in the ditches, curled up in doorways, crawled into abandoned pagan temples, slept in the ruins of Kweilin's shattered homes. During the night, some of those who had fed and rested awhile, moved on, deeper to the south, some farther west, and a few hundred more managed to get on the rice and soup lines; to get something to protect them against the cold. The Monsignor's own coat went to one old man. Wounds were cleaned, bandages put on in place of torn rags that had served for days, in some cases for weeks. Beggars and coolies, rich and middle class, met on the mission lines at common level.

There was no relief from bombing through the Winter, but Monsignor Romaniello's star rode high and bright over Kweilin. The good works of "Monsignor Moonface," were legend not only in Kwangsi, but all along the refugee track. "Get to the Lord of Heaven Man," word went out. "He will feed you and he will tend the sick." The Romaniello good nature didn't break down under the tremendous task presented by unending refugee swarms. The kindnesses at the mission had, by one of the queer twists of war, shown thousands of Chinese the path to God. Grateful men and women wanted to know more about a faith that befriended the poor and the grief-stricken, pagan or Christian. Seated in the dark caves, little groups learned about the Church. Kweilin mission came into its own, but its Prefect did not cease in his tremendous efforts. Fifteen or sixteen hours a day became more or less routine.

On the morning of July 31, 1939, two Japanese bombs burst with a roar in the Maryknoll compound. When the smoke curled up, the chapel and part of the rectory were rubble in a blackened crater. A few hundred feet away another crater, twenty feet across and more than ten feet deep, marked a miss. The air raid warning had come in time. Monsignor Romaniello, his staff and the wounded and hungry were in the caves when the bombs fell. After the all-clear, the Prefect came out of the caverns and stared a long time at the smoking brick. A certain grimness, unusual in his round features, lasted only a little while. Monsignor Romaniello turned away. "We'll start work on a new chapel when they let up a little," he told his staff quietly. He plodded back to the kitchens and feeding was resumed.

Not long after the chapel was destroyed, Monsignor Romaniello was asked to confirm a group of Chinese children in the lovely village of Chemu, about eight miles from Kweilin. It was Moon Festival time, which corresponds, more or less, to the American Thanksgiving. Pomelo trees, instead of pumpkin vines, are heavy then, and the women bake sugary moon cakes. Chemu's harvest had been good. The Prefect left Kweilin after the evening feeding and rode to Chemu in the dark. Firecrackers greeted his arrival. The night was clear, with brittle, glittering stars and, for the first time in days, there was no drone of bombers in the sky. Confirmation was set for next morning.

At sunrise Chemu turned out for the great event, all gaiety and laughter. Forty-three children were prepared for the ceremony, much as they would be at home, mothers and elders fussing and scolding as they herded them toward the village chapel. Only a few had entered when suddenly the bombers' hum worked up to a drumming roar. Sixteen Mitsubishis, arrogant masters of the sky, eight lengthwise, eight across, in perfect formation thundered overhead. The congregation scattered for some banyan trees. They shivered in the trees' shade, protected by its foliage from the planes' observers. The smaller children whimpered, but elders, whispering, hushed them, as if the sound might be heard and bring the bombers back.

Finally, the planes roared past, headed for Kweilin, Monsignor Romaniello called the congregation to Mass and the service was started. The ground trembled as bombs thudded into Kweilin. A few minutes later the concussions came closer. Men, women and children prayed with their hands over their eyes. The forty-three children, moving past the chapel windows for confirmation, saw new fires arising out of Kweilin, thick smoke writhing against the fresh morning heaven. Some of the Chemu peasants wept. Men, women and children were dying in Kweilin. A few bombs plunged into the earth and burst just beyond the chapel. Monsignor Romaniello saw something of panic in the women's eyes. "You must not fear," he told them, calmly. "God is with us."

Pretty soon the bombers' hum died away, temple bells and sirens sounded all-clear. Children and adults escorted the missioner to the tables, the courtyard filled again with childish prattle, but the Prefect was concerned for Kweilin. Chemu's chief man spoke at great length of the days when he had been head man in the village devil's society, before he had taken the Good Road. Monsignor Romaniello listened out of politeness, though he had heard the story fifty times, until he could safely rise and take the road back to Kweilin again. In the city he found more scattered buildings, with rescue parties digging for dead and dying. The refugees were already out of the caves and the rice lines were moving again.

One morning the Prefect stood at Foo River landing, supervising the removal of altars and benches from the compound to a large sampan. Silent Chinese watched coolies carrying these loads to the vessel. For a long time they didn't speak. Finally a native said, "After all, it is not the *Shen Fu's* war. He has stayed with us for almost four years and he has been good to us. It is only right, now, that he should want to return to his own people." A Chinese left this group to say good-bye to Monsignor Moonface. "We understand," he told the Prefect. "It has come time for you to leave. We wish you well for your great kindness." Monsignor Romaniello laughed. "Leave you?" he said. "I'm not leaving. I am setting up new altars on this sampan until we can rebuild the bombed chapel."

Things changed suddenly after this. Mitsubishis and Zeros one morning in 1941 found the skies were not their own. Shark-nosed American P-40's dived on them from great heights in roaring anger, with guns blazing. Zeros were blown apart and Mitsubishis, slow to lumber out of the way, broke in scattered formations. The greater part of a large flight either exploded in the sky, or crashed earthward in flame and black smoke. The Flying Tigers had challenged Japanese air supremacy. Pretty soon legends about the American planes and their pilots were excitably exchanged in Kweilin tea houses and in the streets. The mission compound, still crowded with refugees, cheered the news, and the missioners hungrily ate up the stories just as the Chinese did.

At Wuchow, below Kweilin, in Monsignor Romaniello's former mission territory, the Maryknoll men one morning saw the Tigers tear another Japanese formation to flinders, but when the Americans roared after remnants of the enemy flight which had turned tail, one P-40 stuttered, coughed and wobbled above the rice fields. Father Reilly of Roxbury, Mass., a former Boston College football star, and Father Russell Sprinkle of Middletown, Ohio, watched its descent with bated breath. The river had just receded, after flood, and though it looked solid from the air, silt was three feet deep. A landing on this muck would be disastrous. Someone ran out waving a handkerchief, trying to head off the faltering plane. It developed later that the plane was out of gasoline, its radio dead, and the pilot had no choice.

The plane flattened out, skimmed the rice fields with its wheels scattering spray for hundreds of yards. Suddenly the wheels caught in the mud. The plane balanced crazily on its nose, and slowly turned over like a clumsy man executing a hand-stand and forward flip. The Maryknoll men waded through the muck. Chinese around the compound stared uncertainly for a moment, then the mid-day quiet filled with their shrill cries and they followed. A young American pilot crawled from the cockpit when the priests came up, breathless, prying their feet from the mud at each cumbersome step. The flier had a Chinese-American pocket dictionary in his hand. He was trying to find the Chinese words for, "Get me a drink of water."

The priests passed the request, in voluble Cantonese, and two Chinese boys raced back through the mud to fill it. The flier introduced himself. "I'm Lieutenant Marks, one of Chennault's men," he said. He was strapped to his seat, upside down, when the plane nosed over, but he had suffered no hurt. He said, "I got a bit of a mud bath but otherwise I'm okay." Eager Chinese stripped him of his flying garb right in the rice field, and hurried away with it. The Lieutenant seemed worried about this bold bit of looting until Father Sprinkle reassured him. "They worship your fliers," he told the lieutenant. "All Chinese do. They want the honor of washing your clothes. Your things are safe." One of the Chinese took off his own blue cotton trousers and passed them to the lieutenant.

The flier was wide-eyed at the missioner's glib Cantonese. "How long you been out here?" he inquired. Father Sprinkle said he had ten years in South China. The guest whistled. "I dip my wings to you," he said. "I've put in only a few weeks out here and I'm ready to go back to Bayonne, New Jersey, any time." After a bath and a meal at the mission, the missioners returned to the plane with the flier and interpreted his instructions for dismantling it.

The Japanese might send over a reconnaissance ship any time, the pilot figured, and the sooner it was removed the better. Chinese eagerly followed instructions, took the ship apart, and, chanting, carried the heavy wings, fuselage and motors, through the deep mud to a Chinese junk.

In characteristic Chinese fashion they sang as they proudly bore their load along. "We carry this for the American," they improvised. "He is one whom the Japanese fear. We carry his air devil and the air devil is real." The "air devil" was the fierce looking shark's snout painted on the ship's nose, the insignia of the Flying Tigers. Chinese children splashed in the mud on the plane bearers' flanks reciting little verses of their own. "Ai-yah," they shrilled happily. "Ai-yah. We walk with the air devil." They gave the "thumbs up" high-sign. This was the most exciting event in their lives, something to make parlor conversation forever.

The plane parts were carefully loaded on the junk and covered with tarpaulin. That night the flier was guest of honor at a Chinese banquet, with missioners interpreting the grandiloquent but thoroughly earnest after-dinner speeches which embarrassed Lieutenant Marks with their high praise. Next morning the junk floated down river, with Father Sprinkle aboard as interpreter. There were stops at several Maryknoll missions for food and for rest. It took three days to float the salvaged ship to its base, a distance it could have covered in almost as many minutes at top flying speed. At the end of the journey the lieutenant was grateful to the point of tears. "We didn't know about American missioners in this part of the world," he said. "Next time we're out after our Japanese friends we'll be waving to you." The priests shook his hand. "You might drop a pack of Chesterfields, too," they suggested as they shoved off. "We're out of American cigarettes."

After the United States had entered the war, Chennault's Flying Tigers were dissolved and in June, 1942, a new United States Army Air Corps unit replaced them. The new group had heard, through Air Corps grapevine, that in leisure hours a pilot could go into Kweilin mission for a few hours, talk with the Prefect and the other American missioners, hear American phonograph records and, for a little while anyway, get something of the atmosphere of home. Monsignor Romaniello was always their eager and affable host. The Air Force kids—pilots, bombardiers, gunners—enjoyed the mission's hospitality or wandered Kweilin's streets with the missioners as escorts and interpreters, in the worshipful stare of the Chinese.

On Easter Sunday morning, 1942, Monsignor Romaniello asked Father Joseph Cosgrove, a West Newton, Massachusetts boy, to celebrate Easter Mass at the American airfield. It was a four-hour ride by motorcycle on washboard roads, but Joe Cosgrove knew his mechanical broncho and roared onto the airport with one hand on the handlebars, one raised in greeting. Lieutenant Gregory Carpenter of Keene, N. H., who used to be a magician on New England vaudeville circuits, introduced him to a new batch of airmen, just in from the States. Major Edmond Goss of Tampa, Fla., the commanding officer, came out to shake hands with him. The airport bulletin board had prepared the men for the missioner's coming and the Mass got under way, with airplane motors and roaring jeeps for musical background.

The soldier communicants had barely lifted their heads after the final prayer when the red-ball flag shot up to the field flag pole, first warning of enemy planes in the vicinity. The air was clear, the sun bright. Anti-aircraft gunners on the field's rim jumped to position and scanned the sky. The Japanese were still invisible but word came that they were headed for the airport from the direction of Hankow. Father Cosgrove hurriedly stowed his mission kit, took to one of the hill pits with the ground crew and thrilled as the P-40's burst into deafening clatter, raced down the runways in tremendous clouds of dust, then climbed skyward at astonishing speed. No Japanese were in sight.

A few days before Easter the 23rd Squadron had blown seven Zeros to bits over their home field. This morning, it seemed obvious, the Sons of Heaven were coming out in greater force to avenge that rough handling. The field radio reported twelve Japanese planes coming from the direction of Hankow, fifteen more from the direction of Canton. By this time the shark-snouted American ships had climbed out of sight. Eight minutes after the first warning, Jap formations were visible from the hill pit. They were putting on an air circus—weaving, diving, rolling—in an obvious display of flying skill. A boyish mechanic nudged Father Cosgrove. He said, "They're having fun up there at around seventeen thousand, but just keep your eyes on them."

Bombs came away from the Mitsubishis racks, but they fell outside the field. Father Cosgrove thrilled as the ground shuddered. Suddenly a hideous screaming overwhelmed all other sound. Out of a light cloud, high above the field, the shark-nosed American ships dived on the clowning Zeros at 550 miles an hour. The Japanese fighters glinted in the sun as they left off their aerial horseplay in startled attempt to meet this attack. Chattering P-40 guns exploded one before it got into climbing position. Burning fragments drifted toward the field's eastern rim. Against the sky, where the Zero had been, there was a puff of white smoke, nothing more.

Another Zero blew up on the field's western rim. A third plummeted to earth with a dead Japanese pilot at the stick. The grinning boy mechanic nudged Father Cosgrove again. "Boy, did you see that?" he wanted to know. "Those Japs don't seem to earn a nickel with this bunch." Father Cosgrove was too awed to answer. He saw five enemy aircraft blow up, or death-dive beyond the airport. A Japanese reconnaissance ship streaked over the airdrome dropping pamphlets. Two P-40's dived on this ship's tail. One American pilot loosed a burst, but overshot the target. Behind him, Captain John Hampshire let go another. The air filled with fragments, and again, where the Japanese ship had been limned against the sky, there was only smoke and black-ened fragments turning over and over, like burnt paper.

The scramble lasted fifty-five minutes. By that time the Japanese had scattered and broken off the fight. They had lost five ships, the Americans had lost none. Mechanics picked up the pamphlets the Japanese had scattered. They contained a written challenge to the Americans to come up to fight twelve Zeros. Apparently, the scheme had been for the Americans to concentrate on the flight from Hankow, and while they were engaged in it, the fifteen from Canton were to sneak in and dive on the Americans. "Just bad timing on their part," one of the pilots told the missioner.

A Chinese boy, one of a group of awed urchins who had witnessed the fight, had plunged through the tall grass to the spot where one of the exploded Zeros had landed. The boy came back, bearing a gruesome trophy. It was one of the pilot's arms. "I bear this to the village to show the elders," he said, innocently. A soldier took the thing away from him. Father Cosgrove rode back into Kweilin still aquiver with excitement.

The refugee swarms have all passed now, but they have left a tremendous residue. Kweilin has been rebuilt and its population has tripled. Small Chinese war factories and Government institutions have shot up in and west of the city. Street crowds are far greater now, than when Father Romaniello first took over the haunted house in West Alley. The round foreigner who was looked on with suspicion ten years ago, is a figure of great respect and much face. His chapel, blasted by Japanese bombs, has been rebuilt by eager Chinese artisans, with materials salvaged from other battered structures in the city. Last Christmas the Chinese Catholics at the Monsignor's Mass spilled over into the street because of their great numbers. American airmen still make his mission their favorite spot in town, though Hong Kong refugees have set up enticing tea rooms and restaurants everywhere. On clear nights, Chinese grin affectionately as the Lord of Heaven Man moves down the crowded street, whistling. They don't know the words of the tune, but the song is, "Little Grey Home In The West," and, oddly enough, there is no melancholy, no homesickness in it. It's just Monsignor Moonface's favorite song, the one he sang most back in Fourth Street, New Rochelle.

IX

Under the Rising Sun

EARLY IN THE FALL of 1941 a peculiar restlessness stirred Japan. Maryknoll missioners in both Japan and Korea sensed it because they had spent many years within the Empire and had come to understand the Japanese moods. The missioners noticed how restrictions gradually tightened on all foreigners, particularly Americans. It became difficult, then almost impossible, to travel by rail, a certain sign that Japan was preparing for something extraordinary and was hiding it from strangers within the gates.

Use of the telephone and the telegraph were denied when the messages or voices were English. Inter-island mail came under sharp scrutiny and a letter that should have reached its destination in a day or two, now took a week or more. Uniformed Japanese policemen and Japanese detectives in mufti made a rather clumsy job of turning up at the missions to keep informed. They questioned mission servants, trailed native Christians to and from church, and entered communicants' homes to inquire into the missioners' most innocent routine movements.

Ambassador Grew protested against this excessive gumshoeing which seemed altogether pointless, especially among missioners who confined themselves strictly to clerical duties, but the Japanese, with traditional persistency as well as traditional politeness, were not persuaded. By November of 1941, it was obvious that it did not matter what calling an American followed, the fact that he was American was enough to make him suspect. To men who had spent more than a decade in this milieu the portent became ominously plain. The Japanese were girding for war and were overreaching in their attempts to conceal it.

In November, the missioners found their congregations augmented by Japanese policemen who listened carefully to each word in the sermons and in the prayers. When they heard nothing even remotely bearing on political hostility to Japan, they stopped Japanese Christians in the street and warned them against attending the foreign Church. At this time, incidentally, they had begun to seize papers in all foreigners' homes. Working through house servants, they gained entry to private dwellings and where a letter or a memorandum was beyond their understanding, though it was clearly non-political, the foreigner was apt to be hurried to the police station for questioning.

The men of Maryknoll realized, with the passing weeks, that something important was about to be launched in Japan. Father Everett F. Briggs of Allston, Mass., a Maryknoller who had been in Japan almost ten years, recalls that "a sense of impending disaster weighed heavily on us. We could not undertake the most insignificant activity without the conscious fear that this was likely to be of no avail a short time hence. The tension was indescribable." Father Briggs was stationed at Shiga Ken near Kyoto.

Early on the morning of December 8, in Japan—December 7, in the United States—the Japanese radio hinted with characteristic indirectness, at a naval action in the Pacific. The missioners were stunned. They had feared some military move, but not outright attack without some preliminary. They were uncertain what might follow—but not for long. At the very moment that the broadcasting started, fussy little operatives began entering Americans' homes. Father Briggs and the twelve other Maryknoll men in the neighborhood were on the lists, as well as the small group of Maryknoll Sisters.

Father Briggs' first caller on the morning of December 8 was Mr. Tada, from the Central Police Station. Father Briggs was intent on sermon notes when Tojima San, his Japanese housekeeper, called up the stairs, "A policeman to see you, Father." Her voice quavered nervously. Mr. Tada, though, was coldly polite. He had his hat in his hand and his face was set in hard lines. "You are not to leave these premises today," he announced frigidly. "You are not to go beyond this threshold." Father Briggs wanted to know why. "I shall return," said Mr. Tada, "and you shall be acquainted with the reason."

Mr. Tada was back within the hour. He told the missioner, "There is war between Japan and the United States. If you try to leave this house you might be mobbed by the people in the streets. Under no condition must you leave." Mr. Tada went away. The missioner returned to his sermon notes, but the door opened again. This time it was a group of Japanese air raid wardens. They gave sharp orders for blacking out the house and warned the work must be done at once. Father Briggs went from room to room, after they had gone, blacking the rectory windows and then the windows of the school in the church basement.

Mr. Tada had posted a sentry at the rectory door, to reenforce his orders to the missioner, but Father Briggs had anticipated this. He went calmly on with his routine work and was still at it, at two o'clock the next morning, when he heard the guard sharply challenge a group approaching the house. Lusty hammering on the rectory door awakened the housekeeper. Startled, Tojima San hurried from her bed and opened the door. A little Japanese gendarme and a little Japanese detective faced her. Towering between them was Brother Clement of Maryknoll, a man from St. Mary's, Kansas. The Japanese had taken him from his cot in Kobe Hospital, despite doctors' insistence that he was too ill to be moved. Father Briggs got Brother Clement to bed. The Japanese sentry curled up in the rectory entry to sleep.

Early on the morning of December 11, Father Briggs opened the door to behold a Japanese, somewhat like a dwarf doorman, draped in an unfamiliar uniform rich with military braid, epaulettes and assorted decorations. It was the Chief of the Foreign Section of the Municipal Police. Behind him stood five diminutive detectives. The Chief tried hard to be polite and, in a formal way, was apologetic, but he turned his little men loose in the house and they swarmed through the rooms. They came away triumphantly with religious books, Maryknoll correspondence and all other papers. They frisked Father Briggs and when they found nothing, emptied his wardrobe, turned all his clothing inside out, inspecting even the seams.

With thoroughness and gravity that might have been

amusing under other conditions, they called out everything they found on Father Briggs—one pencil, one fountain pen, a box of matches—as if these were sinister possessions, and their clerical man made corresponding notations. They left with the mission typewriter and all the books and papers, bearing them as though they were secret documents looted from the vaults of the American State Department. The glittering Chief of the Foreign Section bowed himself out. "Sorry," he murmured, "but your country is at war with my country. I must perform this distasteful task. It is my duty." Father Briggs and the ailing Brother Clement were left in a house that looked as though a gale had departed from it after a violent weekend.

Late in the afternoon a cold rain fell in Otsu. The little gendarmes came back again and ordered Father Briggs to move all his personal effects to the church basement. The missioner struggled between the little rectory and the church under loads of bedding, tables, chairs and dishes through a lane of solemn, unblinking gendarmes standing under shiny umbrellas. They had no orders to help, but merely stood like statues in the downpour until all was transferred. The missioner, done at last, dripped with rain.

The church basement, it turned out, had been picked as a temporary internment camp. Father Briggs was hardly settled in it, with Brother Clement shivering because there was no stove to warm the room, before the Japanese ushered in Mr. Van West, an elderly Dutch gentleman, and Father Arthur Merfeld, brought from the Maryknoll house at nearby Karasaki. The gendarmes indicated that the internees were to sleep on the floor. In the early evening another dripping Maryknoll man, Father Clarence Witte of Richmond, Indiana, arrived under military escort. He had been taken from the mission at Hikone.

The little Japanese cook tried to talk with Father Briggs, but the policeman stopped her. "You are now in the employ of the Japanese Government," they told her pompously. The internees were allowed to have their meal in the rectory and then were paraded through the rain to the church basement again. They turned in, shivering with the cold.

The little group came to know the church basement as a prison. They were led from it only for meals. During the brief outdoor periods between basement and rectory, they gulped in the refreshing breeze off Lake Biwa because sometimes the basement grew intolerably damp and stuffy. Mr. Asari, Chief of Provincial Police, showed up one day in full dress uniform, all gold braid and brass buttons, supporting a glittering curved sword, and behind him in equal glory trailed two other little men, likewise with curved swords. "Mr. Roosevelt has made a great mistake," Mr. Asari kept repeating, gleefully. "One great mistake."

Eventually, Mr. Yamanaka, the Chief of the Foreign Section of the Municipal Police, prevailed on Mr. Asari to let the internees get back to the little rectory. The rooms were small there and the men were crowded, but there was heat in the smaller place, and a wash room. The internees spent weeks around the fire, wondering what was taking place about them and far out in the Pacific; what had become of other Maryknoll men in Japan and in Korea. Japanese detectives and Japanese military spies dogged their little housekeeper when she went shopping and eagerly interviewed the butcher and the baker after she had made her purchases. The little housekeeper knew she was followed and her trailers knew she was aware of it. Nothing came of it, but they played the game unflaggingly for so it was written in the books.

After a time, when the tinned foods began to run out, the internees' diet got down to rice, fish, greens and tea, which are Japanese staples but hardly appetizing enough for Westerners. Every item was carefully checked by the guards and the bookkeeping eventually became topheavy and complicated. The cook had to provide two copies of the menu for each meal, stating the amounts of each ingredient used and their approximate price. This seemed to Father Briggs and the other Americans a needless chore, but the more involved the accounts became the more the Japanese found delight in performing what they felt was a service to the Empire.

Tojima San ran into increasing difficulties. The little detectives urged her neighbors to shun her or to try to talk her out of her loyalty to Father Briggs and the other Americans. They harangued her in the streets on her marketing errands. The petty officials talked some of the shopkeepers into refusing to sell her food for the "enemies of Japan" until her daily route, each day, extended farther and farther from the house. Sometimes she came clacking back through the rain in her little wooden shoes, her eyes red with weeping. Father Briggs tried to persuade her, for her own sake, to leave the job. "We'll manage somehow," he assured her, "and we shall not forget your loyalty and courage." But Tojima San wouldn't go.

Throughout this early internment period, the tireless detectives kept working among Father Briggs' parishioners,

even among the Japanese children who had attended his
school. On the few occasions when the missioner got into
the streets, children who used to run, smiling, to meet him,
now scurried out of sight at his approach. Adult parishioners were grilled for eight and ten hours at a stretch in the
hope that they might yield some scrap of information on
which the police might base a pretense for seizing the
Maryknoll properties. The detectives got nowhere at all.

The bamboo wireless, or local grapevine, brought back
to Father Briggs the story of how the detectives had worked
for hours on aged Anna, a withered Japanese Christian.
"Don't you know," the policemen told her, "that this missioner is an enemy of your country?" Old Anna wasn't
caught with this bait. "He is no enemy," she told them
calmly. "It does not matter where he was born, whether it
was Germany, or France or America. I only know him as a
man of God." The detectives tried another tack. "Don't
you know, Old One, that the church was built with American money, and that everything in it came from an enemy
country?" Old Anna kept her withered hands folded patiently in her lap. "The God in that Church did not come
from America," she said. "He is not the God of America
alone, nor of Japan alone. You will find Him in every
country." The police captain gave up. He seemed a little
confused. "You have answered well," he finally decided.
"Thank you, Old One." Old Anna clumped out.

Father Briggs was touched by these stories and a great
indignation welled up in him. He came to feel that he
must do something in his flock's behalf. "As things stood,"
he explains, "it was impossible to break through the screen
of official secrecy by ordinary methods. As for extraor-

dinary methods, there was little choice. I resolved on a hunger strike. If Gandhi could do it for India, I figured, I could do it for the Kingdom of Heaven."

At the end of the first week's fast, Mr. Asari of the gilt braid and gilt buttons, showed up. He didn't seem to know what to do in this unusual situation. Suddenly, though, he drew himself up, pointed significantly to the chrysanthemum emblem (gilded) on his visored military cap. "I must charge you," he blustered, "with opposing the policy of the Japanese Government. You are guilty of high treason to His Majesty, the Emperor." Father Briggs knew that to a simple Japanese peasant these words would spell swift and pitiless punishment, but he recognized them for so much bluster.

"I charge you," he told Mr. Asari quietly, "with violating the laws of His Majesty the Emperor which guarantee the rights of the Church." His lips were dry and his throat was parched from the fast, and the little speech was weirdly harsh.

The missioner's reaction startled Mr. Asari's brilliantly-uniformed assistants. Father Briggs saw them shudder. It isn't good form to tell off a high official of the Emperor's police. Mr. Asari was embarrassed to find that the conventional official procedure hadn't frightened the missioner.

Mr. Asari finally thought of a retort.

He said, "Are all Americans like you?"

The missioner said, "I dare say a great many are."

Mr. Asari's *wet-grape* eyes glinted.

"Then why do they go on strikes and halt their country's war production?" he asked triumphantly. This seemed, in his opinion, to have restored lost face. He executed a smart turnabout and stamped away, his lieutenants stamping behind him.

Nevertheless, Father Briggs' stratagem had worked. Native assistants who had been jailed for refusing to say falsely that the missioner was an active enemy of Japan, were released. The church was reopened and the keys were turned over to the Japanese Prefect Apostolic, Monsignor Furuya of Kyoto. Father Briggs, meanwhile, had overtaxed himself. He was in bed six weeks as a result of the fast.

The police licked their wounds from this encounter, but only for a little while. They finally came up with the idea that Father Briggs be transferred from his own rectory to a centuries-old Buddhist temple nearby, which they—and the missioner—knew, was verminous and rat-infested. "You're better treated here," they told him, "than our nationals are in the internment camps in the United States." But Father Briggs escaped transfer to the temple. He and the other Maryknoll missioners were put, instead, on the list for removal to an internment camp in Kobe.

Father Briggs was anxious to reward Tojima San for her faithfulness and devotion, but the parish funds by that time were near exhaustion. He gave her a full year's salary, which is pitifully little in American dollars, and signed over to her every bit of kitchen equipment including all the shiny pots, pans and skillets. Tojima San was tearfully grateful. She said, "I will cherish them. I will take the best care of them." The missioners were allowed two bags each, but the ubiquitous little detectives inspected every item that went into the luggage.

One item specially interested them. It was a tiny bundle

rolled in pure white silk. "One flag," said Father Briggs, and prepared to put it in the bag. The detectives were suspicious. "What flag?" they wanted to know. Father Briggs said, "My country's flag." They insisted on seeing it. The missioner knew that in Japan, anything sacred is rolled in precious silk and is never disclosed without formal ceremony. He started to peel the silk covering in the impressive Japanese manner. He said, "This will take time. This item is precious," but the little detectives still wanted to see it. Father Briggs prolonged the process until the stars and stripes lay exposed. He handled the flag tenderly. One of the detectives said, "It is a very pretty flag," but the other detective seemed irritated. "All right," he said, crisply, and Father Briggs reverently re-rolled the banner in the silk covering.

"I had gone to Japan as a priest rather than as an American," he likes to relate, "but I felt I should give these men a demonstration of loyalty to my country. The significance of my handling of the flag with such elaborate ceremony was not lost on the Shiga police."

The police allowed the missioners to say Mass in the church at Shiga Ken the last three days before their departure for Kobe. Japanese guards, however, surrounded the building. Only a few parishioners got through to attend these Masses, but on the morning when the missioners left for the station, a little queue of Japanese women and children clumped after them, heedless of the scowling soldier and police escort. Father Briggs' throat was lumped with emotion as he looked back on the cobalt roof of his little church, lighted by morning sun, on the trees, on the neat green lawns, and on the tidy grove beyond.

More terrorized parishioners peeped from their windows
as the missioners moved slowly down the street into exile.
In the station, when the train rolled in, three Japanese
women braved the guards again. Tears crystallized in their
eyes and Father Briggs fought to keep the tears from well-
ing up in his. The women and their little girls bowed and
their lips moved. The missioner heard them murmur,
"*Sayonara*," the Japanese farewell. "*Sayonara*," he called
back to them, brokenly, but the guards were gruff. "Let's
go," they said in their native tongue. As the train got under
way, Father Briggs could still see the little knot of faithful
women and children. Their heads were still bent in prayer.

A few hours later the missioners were tenants in the
Eastern Lodge at Kobe, a cheap wooden hotel with some
forty tiny rooms which had formerly housed some Parsees,
and still—nominally, at least—run by an Indian. The ac-
tual custodian was Mr. Ee, a rather kindly gaffer who had
been a Japanese sergeant of police. Mr. Ee was small and
his bald head was like a copper ball. There were some English refugees, some Dutch, Canadians, Belgians, two Guate-
malans, one Australian and six American women who had
been brought from Guam. The missioners got up Japanese
language classes, the women played bridge or other card
games.

One day Father Briggs sat in the Eastern Lodge gardens
with Willi, a young Dutchman who had lost his business in
Japan. They talked of the possibility that American air
strength might, eventually, reach the point of sending
bombing squadrons to Tokyo. The Dutchman was skeptical.
"It's a long hop for any bird," he told the missioner
moodily, "because there's no place, now, where he can stop

and scratch his wings, so to speak. I don't think even your American eagle could make it, non-stop." Father Briggs earnestly told Willi he was wrong. "The eagle will come, never doubt it," he said. Willi shook his head, and went inside. Father Briggs was alone in the garden.

Only a few minutes later, by weird coincidence, the missioner heard a motor drone in the sky. He ignored it, at first, thought that the sound merely signalled the approach of a flight of Japanese Mitsubishis, or Zeros, but something impelled him to look upward.

"I thought my imagination had got the better of me," he said later. "A big, stream-lined plane roared into sight, scarcely fifty feet above the elevated railroad. It seemed only rifle-shot away. I knew, as if by telepathy, that the brave men in that silver, fish-like bird heading toward the sea were of my country. I was thrilled to the core of my being. I wanted to wave to them, but almost in the same instant they were gone."

Father Briggs had noticed American insignia on the bomber's fuselage, the star of the American Army Air Force. His heart pounded with excitement. His impulse was to cry out to the other internees, but discretion saved him. He simply stared like a man in a dream as the bomber roared out of sight. Then he heard the sound of fallen bombs. He counted them—one, two, three. "I prayed," he remembers, "that no innocent soul had suffered harm from them." Eastern Lodge shook under the bombs' impact as the explosives landed on railroad yards in Kobe. Smoke writhed up from the spot. Father Briggs stared, fascinated.

Angry Japanese sentries rushed into the garden. They ordered the missioner indoors. The little men were visibly upset but they did not tell the prisoners that American bombers had been over Kobe, over Tokyo and over other parts of Japan. The internees were to learn more than a year afterward that these squadrons had taken off from the flight deck of an American carrier, and had carried out their mission under General James Doolittle.

"We knew, though, that a tremor of secret fear ran through Japan," Father Briggs said. "If the eagle could come once, he could come again. What other emotions stirred in the breasts of the Japanese we did not know, but we could guess. From that night, onward, every night, our quarters were blacked out. We were not allowed out of doors during air-raid alarms. We were forbidden to so much as look at any passing plane."

Maryknoll men exiled from their missions in Manchuria and in Korea, eventually came to Kobe and to Yokohama. On June 9, 1942, Father Briggs got word that Father Leo Peloquin of Brockton, Mass., who had served in Korea, lay dying in the hospital in Kobe. A Miss Meyers, a Presbyterian nurse, had attended him on the long journey from his mission and had remained by his cot in Kobe. "I guess," Father Peloquin told Father Briggs, "I'll have to take the next repatriation boat. I won't make this one." Next morning, just before noon, Father Peloquin whispered to Miss Meyers. "Miss Meyers," he began, "I wonder—." He never finished. His boat had come, and it had borne him off. He is buried on a green hill in Kobe.

Father Peloquin had been in Korea seventeen years. He was only one of a large force of men of Maryknoll who had loved that country, The Land of Morning Calm. Father Leo Sweeney, brother of Big Joe who runs the leper colony at Heaven's Gate, had labored there for many years before the Japanese sent him into exile with all the rest. Father Sweeney and Father Pospichal had established a center of the apostolate in Chinnampo that had become the perfect symbol of a Maryknoll mission. His sympathetic writings of the Korean elders in his old folks' home who had come upon misfortune, had touched countless hearts in the United States.

Among these wards and parishioners were withered men and women well into their eighties, some in their nineties, who had been left to die until he brought them into his warm shelter and fed them. Even pagan Koreans and Japanese contributed to the home and came to respect all men of Maryknoll because of it. One of the inmates of the home was an aged carver who had earned his living by wandering from village to village, fashioning pagan idols. After Father Sweeney had picked him up exhausted, one day, the carver decided he would repay the kindness by carving a life-size figure of Christ. He had all but finished it, an exquisite work, when he died; "Chiseled his way into Heaven," to hear Father Sweeney tell it.

Father Leo J. Steinbach of Chariton, Iowa, was exiled from Korea, too, after his good works had become legends. He had saved blind, decrepit Korean beggars, whom he had found dying in the highways; had brought them to his stations and had fed them and clothed them. Certain of the Japanese, who control Korea, were inclined to frown on this work at first, but they realized at last that there was no motive behind it but pity for the weak and neglected. One Buddhist, originally of the protesting group, swung to the other extreme after he had investigated and observed the kindly treatment Father Steinbach gave the beggars. This man contributed a considerable sum to the work and offered to go in the padre's place should the Japanese authorities insist on arresting him. The Japanese dropped the matter.

A legendary figure in the Korean contingent sent into exile by the events of Pearl Harbor, was mild-mannered Father Hubert M. Pospichal, a South Dakotan of saintly bearing, whose handling of children was extraordinary. Father Pospichal wandered in the scrubby alleys of Chinnampo waterfront, picking up little boys and girls for his "Sunset Academy," a primary school where he taught reading and writing. Hundreds of Korean children whose parents never dreamed these attainments possible for their offspring, came to worship the South Dakota farmer with the lovable smile and great hands. Father Pospichal never walked the streets of Chinnampo without whole troops of Korean children shrilling all about him. He was known to other men of Maryknoll as, "The Pied Piper of Chinnampo."

These men, heavy-hearted over their forced departure from the Land of Morning Calm, most peaceful and most fruitful mission field within Maryknoll's Asiatic jurisdiction, joined Father Briggs and other missioners from Japan, at Yokohama. They boarded first the Japanese liner *Asama Maru*, then transferred to the *Gripsholm*, and at last saw New York Harbor one morning at dawn, seventy days after they had set out from Japan. Men and women repatriates crowded against the rail to stare happily at the Statue of Liberty.

"Our eyes were moist," Father Briggs sometimes recalls,

"and I think that many of us felt, for the first time, the true force of Scott's words:

> Breathes there the man with soul so dead,
> Who never to himself hath said,
> This is my own, my native land.

Good! Truly, every man whose heart beats right feels it beat more quickly as he draws near home. But in these men of Maryknoll, there remained a dull, hungry ache beneath the exultation. They were home and yet they were in exile, exiled from their people of predilection on the other side of the earth.

For they were not of one land alone; they, missioners, were the property of all, instruments of the witchery and folly of the Cross for the fulfillment of the great Christian ideal: "There is neither Jew nor Greek, there is neither bond nor free, for we are all one in Christ Jesus."

X

In Bataan Fox Holes

WHEN FATHER WILLIAM THOMAS CUMMINGS asked the
commandant at Manila the evening of December 7, 1941,
to send him with the troops as chaplain, the harassed
officer tried to talk him out of it. "You're not fit," he said,
gruffly. "You're thirty-nine and you're nursing a back injury. You'd be no good for field duty." The missioner,
lean, almost cadaverous, fairly leaped at him. His vehe-
ment speech ended only when he ran out of breath. The
usually calm Cummings stare had something of fierceness
in it. Even in that tense hour the officer was grimly amused.
He said, "Okay, Father. It's good to hear fighting words.
We can use men like you." In a few hours the Maryknoll
missioner had changed his cassock for the uniform and ornaments of a first lieutenant and had joined the band of Catholic and Protestant chaplains bound for Bataan.

Within two months Lieut. Bill Cummings was part of
Philippine Army legend. In spite of the back injury that
had kept him off his feet for more than a year and despite
the disadvantage of a rather slight build and defective
eyesight, he achieved near-miracles during the defense of
Bataan and Corregidor. The few who saw him in action

there and came away to tell it, still glow when they speak of him. He managed, somehow, despite his handicaps, to get along with even less sleep than the thousands of exhausted kids who held off the Japanese against staggering odds, long after anyone believed it possible. He stayed on with his fellow chaplains when the Japanese at last crashed through, over thousands of their own dead.

Perhaps the story is a little stale, now, but Bataan approximated hell on earth, if any place ever did. After three months, the American and Filipino soldiers were fighting on borrowed time. Their fox holes were knee deep in filth and the blistering tropical sun made them bitterly aware of it. Flies swarmed about them in clouds through long hours of daylight, giant mosquitoes plagued them by night. The air was putrid with gangrenous odor and with the stifling stench from uniforms long unwashed, from tortured and sweating bodies too long unbathed. The gray dust kicked up by incessant aerial bombing coated men's faces with a powdery mask. Lips were sealed by mucous and there was scarcely enough water to crack the seal.

Lieutenant Cummings crawled, day after day, from one fox hole to another under intense shell and aerial fire to absolve and anoint, to help get out the wounded, to lie alongside dying boys and murmur words of consolation as they drifted into merciful death or lapsed unconscious. They liked and understood him because he was not the sanctimonious type, but just another soldier, as they were. He went to all alike; nationality didn't matter, nor creed. It was Lieutenant Cummings, according to Colonel Carlos Romulo who was with him on Bataan, who first said, "There are no Atheists in fox holes." His cross collar ornaments seemed to attract snipers' fire, and the men and some of the nurses begged him to take them off. He didn't think it was a good idea. He kept them on to the end.

At night, when Pacific moonlight glinted on bayonets in the fox holes, Lieutenant Cummings still went his tireless rounds, crawling toward where some dying kid screamed or thrashed about in agony. His canteen went to feverish lips, his thin fingers held the delirious down in the shallow shelters. His bent ear caught hundreds of confessions and messages meant for mothers, sisters, wives and brothers these kids would never see again. Before he would lie down among the living and the dead for a few hours of rest, he'd scribble hasty notes or brief letters with these last words written into them. Some of them got out, but probably most of them did not, because their bearers died before they could hand them on.

At night, when stars seemed close enough to touch and Japanese batteries were not kicking up the peninsula's dust in choking clouds, soldiers liked to talk to Lieutenant Cummings about home and school, about city streets alive and alight and filled with laughing people, of village streets serene and quiet at this hour. They lived on a small ration of boiled rice and part of a can of salmon. Their coffee, when it reached them, was bitter. Sometimes the talk would break off and machine guns would stutter and explode in their ears as they thought they detected Japanese creeping in the jungle, or down by the barbed wire on the beach.

The padre knew how their hearts were torn by cunning broadcasts from invisible Japanese sound trucks, hidden in the jungle, that played recordings of "Home Sweet

Home" and "In The Gloaming" to torture them, and he overlooked it when they damned the enemy. Under the Philippine sky he set up a crude altar, a shaky structure of green bamboo with an oily transport corps garage board for table and conducted the Sunday service from it. American and Filipino boys, enlisted men and officers, their rifles, grenades and other deadly paraphernalia ready formed his haggard congregation. The words of the Mass sounded clear above the scream of shells, the earth-shaking explosion of aerial bombs and the frightened chatter of the monkeys.

At least once a day Lieutenant Cummings went from bed to bed in the Base Hospital to talk with the wounded and the fever-stricken. The hospital was hardly more than a great jungle shed with palm fronds for a roof. The sides were open. Hot sun stuck sharp golden spears through the bamboo frame. Sometimes monkeys came down from the tall trees just outside, to stare with roving, bead-like eyes at the patients tossing on the soiled white cots, or lying deathly still in the incessant bedlam. Nurses, driven to superhuman effort, would lead the chaplain to the worst cases first. When bombs shook the ground and cots shuddered, the nurses and the padre would stand by the shell-shocked to still their terror.

For three months Lieutenant Cummings followed this routine. Bombs destroyed one altar after another, but he patiently set up new ones. In March he put through a cable to his mother, back in San Francisco. It said, "Feeling fine. Think of you frequently. Don't worry." This was to be the last direct word from him, but Mrs. Cummings didn't know that.

Late in March, when wounded were coming in at the rate of 1500 a week, many of them amputation cases and bad body wounds, Japanese fliers roared low and bombed the Bataan hospital. The death toll was sickening. A Japanese broadcast from General Homma's headquarters several days later, apologized for this bombing, said it had not been intentional. The nurses seemed to feel a little better after the broadcast and word got around to the wounded that they would probably be spared any further bombing in their cots. There was hardly more than a grain of comfort in this news, though. The doctors had run out of disinfectant and ether and there was no respite from the fly swarms and mosquitoes. Odors were almost unbearable.

On the morning of April 4, a Saturday, Lieutenant Cummings came up from the fox holes on his way to the hospital to arrange details for Easter Sunday Mass in the wards. It was around ten o'clock. The sun burned down fiercely and Japanese shelling was particularly intense. Juanita Redmond, a South Carolina girl and Willa Hook of Renfrow in Oklahoma, both lieutenants in the Nurse Corps, looked up wearily from their tasks to greet the chaplain, ready to point out the morning's critical cases. At that moment, the sudden roar of diving planes brought them to a momentary standstill. A powerful detonation filled the air with a tremendous flash of red flame. Smoke burst from the shattered concrete flooring and shrapnel pinged on the cot frames, drummed on the bamboo walls.

A monstrous cloud of dust rose from the crater and darkened the ward. Powdery earth rained on the stunned wounded, on the nurses and doctors. At almost the same moment a second, even more terrifying explosion, made the earth leap. The doctors, nurses, and Lieutenant Cummings were hurled into the air about two or three feet, and another great belch of flame roared through the open walls. It carried fragments of sand, gravel and shrapnel at screaming velocity. The bomb had touched off a passing ammunition truck. Guards at the hospital entrance were blown into the trees and hung from branches, grotesquely torn. Some patients were hurled thirty to forty yards with their cots.

For a split second silence prevailed, the silence that follows terrifying disaster. Then amputation cases and shell-shock patients were seized with panic. Men without limbs tried to escape outdoors. They were like broken statues covered with marble dust. Legless men tried to roll toward the open walls to get out of the building. The great awning sagged and billowed as if to engulf them. The screams and moans of men cut by new wounds, made the air hideous. Overhead, continuous runs of Japanese Mitsubishis, tearing through anti-aircraft fire, still dropped explosives, each bomb shaking the ground and moving cots out of place.

Doctors and nurses got slowly to their feet. They were dizzy. Their ears rang with explosion aftersound. Lieutenant Cummings stood up. He saw wounded trying to make for outdoors, men writhing in sheer panic. Outside the danger now was worse than in the hospital. He could hear the screams of new victims shrilling through the air. He shook his head as if to clear it, righted a chair and got up on it. Dust lay in smoky strata in the long room, but the hospital staff and some of the men saw his arms upraised. He spoke clearly. He said, "That was a tough one, fellows. Lie quiet where you are. Let's pray." Something in the voice drew instant obedience. Screaming lessened and some of the writhing stopped.

Lieutenant Cummings spoke above the roar of another diving plane, "Our Father Who art in Heaven . . ." From positions on the floor, from dust-covered nurses wiping at bloody faces with sheets and pillow cases there came murmured response—"Our Father Who art in Heaven . . ." Bombs shook the hospital again and Lieutenant Cummings swayed on the chair, but his voice stayed steady. "—Hallowed be Thy Name." The last notes of panic and fright choked off. "Hallowed be Thy Name" came from 200 steadying throats. Repeated concussions, the slatting awning were clearly audible, and a bomber dived again with rising crescendo. "Thy Kingdom come," the chaplain intoned.

Now those who had knees were on them. Dusty-faced men and women, looked toward the tall thin man on the chair with arms still uplifted. "Thy will be done on earth as it is in Heaven." Again the hospital rocked but now there were no frightened screams. Movement toward escape had stopped. A trickle of blood started from under the lieutenant's dark hair and coursed down his forehead. He closed his eyes to shut it out and went on to the end— "and lead us not into temptation, but deliver us from evil . . . Amen." From the upheaved concrete flooring, from the cots and from the dust-covered lips of the doctors and nurses burst, like a communal sigh, a deep "Amen."

Lieutenant Cummings got down from the chair. Doctors and nurses returned abruptly to their tasks. Fifty patients lay dead in the wards, all covered with bomb dust. More than 150 had new wounds, yet the sounds of panic had ended. A kind of peace had come as anodyne. The doctors bustled from bed to bed, righting men shaken to the floor. Nurses and orderlies picked up the amputation cases that had been thrown to the concrete. Stained, sweating features were tenderly wiped with sheets and with toweling. Lieutenant Cummings gently tapped a sunken-eyed nurse as she was about to pass. He said, "Sis, when you get a chance, will you put a tourniquet on my arm." Blood poured from a deep shrapnel wound in his right arm and shoulder.

Next morning, at sunrise, Lieutenant Cummings held Easter Sunday Mass at a makeshift altar under a burning sky. It was his last service on Bataan. Most of the nurses got across to Corregidor in small boats, with ugly-snouted sharks cutting the waves beside them. The sharks had fed to disgusting size since the fighting had started in January. The doctors and nurses tried to get Lieutenant Cummings into one of the crowded boats but he shook his head. "Got a job to do," he told them, smiling. He chose to remain with the troops and other chaplains who were to be prizes of the enemy. The last time they saw him he had turned and vanished among the swarms of ghostly soldiers trying for Corregidor. The Japanese had broken through. Almost a year later word came through that Lieutenant Cummings was a prisoner of war. "Am quite well," he wrote placidly.